THE OPEN FAIR™ BODY OF KN(

The Open Group Publications available from Van Haren Publishing

The TOGAF Series:
TOGAF® Version 9.1
TOGAF® Version 9.1 – A Pocket Guide
TOGAF® 9 Foundation Study Guide, 3rd Edition
TOGAF® 9 Certified Study Guide, 3rd Edition

The Open Group Series:
Cloud Computing for Business – The Open Group Guide
ArchiMate® 2.1 – A Pocket Guide
ArchiMate® 2.1 Specification
ArchiMate® 2 Certification – Study Guide

The Open Group Security Series:
Open Information Security Management Maturity Model (O-ISM3)
Open Enterprise Security Architecture (O-ESA)
Risk Management – The Open Group Guide
The Open FAIR™ Body of Knowledge – A Pocket Guide

All titles are available to purchase from:
www.opengroup.org
www.vanharen.net
and also many international and online distributors.

The Open FAIR™ Body of Knowledge

A POCKET GUIDE

A Taxonomy and Method for Risk Analysis

Prepared by Andrew Josey et al.

THE
Open
GROUP

Van Haren
PUBLISHING

Title:	The Open FAIR™ Body of Knowledge – A Pocket Guide
Subtitle:	A Taxonomy and Method for Risk Analysis
A publication of:	The Open Group
Authors:	Andrew Josey et al.
Publisher:	Van Haren Publishing, Zaltbommel, www.vanharen.net
ISBN Hard copy:	978 94 018 0018 1
ISBN eBook:	978 94 018 0561 2
ISBN ePub:	978 94 018 0562 9
Edition:	First edition, first impression, November 2014
Layout and Cover design:	CO2 Premedia, Amersfoort-NL
Copyright:	© 2014 The Open Group

The views expressed in this Pocket Guide are not necessarily those of any particular member of The Open Group.

In the event of any discrepancy between text in this document and the official Open FAIR documentation, the Open FAIR documentation remains the authoritative version for certification, testing by examination, and other purposes. The official Open FAIR documentation can be obtained online at www.opengroup.org/certifications/openfair.

The Open FAIR® Body of Knowledge – A Pocket Guide

Document Number: G144

Comments relating to the material contained in this document may be submitted to:
The Open Group
Apex Plaza, Forbury Road
Reading
Berkshire, RG1 1AX
United Kingdom

or by electronic mail to: ogspecs@opengroup.org

Preface

This Document

This document is the Pocket Guide for the Open FAIR Body of Knowledge. It is designed to provide a reference for Risk Analysts.

The Open FAIR Body of Knowledge provides a taxonomy and method for understanding, analyzing, and measuring information risk. The outcomes are more cost-effective information risk management, greater credibility for the information security profession, and a foundation from which to develop a scientific approach to information risk management. This allows organizations to:

- Speak in one language concerning their risk
- Consistently study and apply risk analysis principles to any object or asset
- View organizational risk in total
- Challenge and defend risk decisions

The audience for this Pocket Guide is:

- Individuals who require a basic understanding of the Open FAIR Body of Knowledge
- Professionals who are working in roles associated with a risk analysis project, such as those responsible for information system security planning, execution, development, delivery, and operation
- Risk analysts who are looking for a first introduction to the Open FAIR Body of Knowledge

A prior knowledge of risk analysis is advantageous but not required.

The Pocket Guide is structured as follows:

- Chapter 1 (Introduction) provides an introduction to the Open FAIR Body of Knowledge.

- Chapter 2 (Basic Risk Analysis Concepts) introduces the basic concepts of risk analysis.
- Chapter 3 (Risk Taxonomy) describes the Open FAIR taxonomy of terms used for risk analysis.
- Chapter 4 (Risk Terminology) describes the terminology of risk analysis.
- Chapter 5 (Measurement) describes how risk analysis can be best measured.
- Chapter 6 (Risk Analysis Process) describes the process of risk analysis.
- Chapter 7 (Risk Analysis Results) describes how to develop and interpret Open FAIR risk analysis results.

Conventions Used in this Pocket Guide

The following conventions are used throughout this Pocket Guide in order to help identify important information and avoid confusion over the intended meaning.

- Ellipsis (…)

  Indicates a continuation; such as an incomplete list of example items, or a continuation from preceding text.

- **Bold**

  Used to highlight specific terms.

- *Italics*

  Used for emphasis. May also refer to other external documents.

About The Open Group

The Open Group is a global consortium that enables the achievement of business objectives through IT standards. With more than 400 member organizations, The Open Group has a diverse membership that spans all sectors of the IT community – customers, systems and solutions suppliers, tool vendors, integrators, and consultants, as well as academics and researchers – to:

- Capture, understand, and address current and emerging requirements, and establish policies and share best practices

- Facilitate interoperability, develop consensus, and evolve and integrate specifications and open source technologies
- Offer a comprehensive set of services to enhance the operational efficiency of consortia
- Operate the industry's premier certification service

Further information on The Open Group is available at www.opengroup.org.

The Open Group publishes a wide range of technical documentation, most of which is focused on development of Open Group Standards and Guides, but which also includes white papers, technical studies, certification and testing documentation, and business titles. Full details and a catalog are available at www.opengroup.org/bookstore.

Readers should note that updates – in the form of Corrigenda – may apply to any publication. This information is published at www.opengroup.org/corrigenda.

About the Authors

Andrew Josey, The Open Group

Andrew Josey is Director of Standards within The Open Group. He is currently managing the standards process for The Open Group, and has recently led the standards development projects for the ArchiMate 2.1 Specification and the TOGAF 9.1 Standard, IEEE Std 1003.1 2013 Edition (POSIX), and the core specifications of the Single UNIX Specification, Version 4. He is a member of the IEEE, USENIX, UKUUG, and the Association of Enterprise Architects (AEA).

Jack Jones, CISSP, CISM, CISA

Jack Jones has specialized in information security and risk management for 21 years. During this time, he has worked in the US military, government intelligence, consulting, as well as the financial and insurance industries. Jack has over eight years of experience as a CISO, with five of those years at a Fortune 100 financial services company. His work there was recognized in 2006 when he received the 2006 RSA/ISSA Excellence in the Field of Security Practices award. In 2007, he was selected as a finalist for the Information Security Executive of the Year, Central US, and in 2012 was honored with the CSO Compass award for leadership in risk management. He is also the author and creator of the Factor Analysis of Information Risk (FAIR) framework.

Jim Hietala, The Open Group

Jim Hietala, CISSP, GSEC, Open FAIR Certified Risk Analyst, is Vice President, Security for The Open Group, where he manages all security and risk management programs and standards activities, including the Security Forum. He has participated in the development of numerous industry standards including the Risk Taxonomy (O-RT) standard, Risk Analysis (O-RA) standard, O-ISM3, and O-ACEML. He also led the development of The Open Group FAIR Certification Program. He holds a BS in Marketing from Southern Illinois University, and holds three technical security certifications, GSEC-Gold from GIAC/SANS, CISSP from ISC2, and Open FAIR from The Open Group.

Trademarks

Acknowledgements

The Open Group gratefully acknowledges:

- Past and present members of The Open Group Security Forum for developing the Open FAIR Body of Knowledge.
- CXOWARE Inc., for their valued original work, which we have drawn on in preparation of this Study Guide.
- The following reviewers of this document:
  - Steve Else
  - Bill Estrem
  - Jack Freund
  - Chad Weinman

References

The following documents are referenced in this Pocket Guide:

- *How to Measure Anything: Finding the Value of Intangibles in Business*, Douglas W. Hubbard, John Wiley & Sons, 2010.
- *Open Group Guide: FAIR – ISO/IEC 27005 Cookbook* (C103), published by The Open Group, November 2010; refer to www.opengroup.org/bookstore/catalog/c103.htm.
- *Open Group Guide: Requirements for Risk Assessment Methodologies* (G081), published by The Open Group, January 2009; refer to www.opengroup.org/bookstore/catalog/g081.htm.
- *Open Group Standard: Risk Analysis* (O-RA) (C13G), published by The Open Group, October 2013; refer to www.opengroup.org/bookstore/catalog/c13g.htm.
- *Open Group Standard: Risk Taxonomy* (O-RT), Version 2.0 (C13K), published by The Open Group, October 2013; refer to www.opengroup.org/bookstore/catalog/c13k.htm.

The following web links are referenced in this Pocket Guide:

- The Open Group Risk Management information website; refer to www.opengroup.org/subjectareas/security/risk.

Chapter 1
Introduction

This Pocket Guide provides a first introduction to the Open FAIR Body of Knowledge. It will be of interest to individuals who require a basic understanding of the Open FAIR Body of Knowledge, and professionals who are working in roles associated with a risk analysis project, such as those responsible for information system security planning, execution, development, delivery, and operation.

This chapter provides an introduction to the Open FAIR Body of Knowledge.

Topics addressed in this chapter include:
- An Introduction to risk analysis and the Open FAIR Body of Knowledge
- The need for an accurate model and taxonomy
- A simple risk analysis scenario
- The benefits of using the Open FAIR Body of Knowledge
- The constituent parts of the Open FAIR Body of Knowledge
- The relationship of Open FAIR to other Open Group standards and to other risk frameworks and methodologies

1.1 An Introduction to Risk Analysis and the Open FAIR

The Open FAIR Body of Knowledge provides a taxonomy (see Chapter 3) and method (see Chapter 5, Chapter 6, and Chapter 7) for understanding, analyzing, and measuring information risk. It allows organizations to:
- Speak in one language concerning their risk using the standard taxonomy and terminology

- Consistently study and apply risk analysis principles to any object or asset
- View organizational risk in total
- Challenge and defend risk decisions

What does FAIR stand for?
FAIR is an acronym for Factor Analysis of Information Risk.

1.1.1 Risk Analysis: The Need for an Accurate Model and Taxonomy

Organizations seeking to analyze and manage risk encounter some common challenges. Put simply, it is difficult to make sense of risk without having a common understanding of both the factors that (taken together) contribute to risk, and the relationships between those factors. The Open FAIR Body of Knowledge provides such a taxonomy.

Here's an example that will help to illustrate why a standard taxonomy is important. Let's assume that you are an information security risk analyst tasked with determining how much risk your company is exposed to from a "lost or stolen laptop" scenario. The degree of risk that the organization experiences in such a scenario will vary widely depending on a number of key factors. To even start to approach an analysis of the risk posed by this scenario to your organization, you will need to answer a number of questions, such as:

- Whose laptop is this?
- What data resides on this laptop?
- How and where did the laptop get lost or stolen?
- What security measures were in place to protect the data on the laptop?
- How strong were the security controls?

The level of risk to your organization will vary widely based upon the answers to these questions. The degree of overall organizational risk posed by lost laptops must also include an estimation of the frequency of occurrence of lost or stolen laptops across the organization.

In one extreme, suppose the laptop belonged to your CTO, who had IP stored on it in the form of engineering plans for a revolutionary product in a significant new market. If the laptop was unprotected in terms of security controls, and it was stolen while he was on a business trip to a country known for state-sponsored hacking and IP theft, then there is likely to be significant risk to your organization. On the other extreme, suppose the laptop belonged to a junior salesperson a few days into their job, it contained no customer or prospect lists, and it was lost at a security checkpoint at an airport. In this scenario, there's likely to be much less risk. Or consider a laptop which is used by the head of sales for the organization, who has downloaded Personally Identifiable Information (PII) on customers from the CRM system in order to do sales analysis, and has his or her laptop stolen. In this case, there could be Primary Loss to the organization, and there might also be Secondary Losses associated with reactions by the individuals whose data is compromised.

The Open FAIR Body of Knowledge is designed to help you to ask the right questions to determine the asset at risk (is it the laptop itself, or the data?), the magnitude of loss, the skill level and motivations of the attacker, the resistance strength of any security controls in place, the frequency of occurrence of the threat and of an actual loss event, and other factors that contribute to the overall level of risk for any specific risk scenario.

1.1.2 Scenario – A Bald Tire

We will look in detail at the Open FAIR taxonomy and method in subsequent chapters, starting with the risk taxonomy that enables us to speak in one language concerning risk. Before we do that we use the following scenario as a first introduction to some of the key concepts of risk analysis.

1. Consider a scenario of a bald tire; it is so bald you can hardly see any tread on it. How much risk is associated with that tire?
2. The tire is now hanging from a rope attached to a tree. How much risk is there?
3. You notice that the rope attached to the tree is badly frayed. How much risk is there?
4. The bald tire is hanging from the badly frayed rope over the edge of a cliff with jagged rocks at the bottom.

What are the threats, vulnerabilities, and risk within this scenario?

Many readers assume that the risk is highest in 4. The answer, however, is that there is very little probability of significant loss given the scenario as described. Who cares that an empty, old bald tire falls to the rocks below? Many readers assume that someone will climb up and swing on the tire. This is a reasonable assumption and illustrates that assumptions are easy to make when performing a risk analysis. Unexamined assumptions about key aspects of the risk environment can seriously weaken an analysis.

A first point we take away from this scenario is that the risk landscape is so complex that we must make assumptions – there will always be assumptions in any analysis. What is most important when using the Open FAIR method is that we document, examine, and challenge our assumptions to ensure we can effectively communicate and defend our results.

The second point from this scenario is that multiple readers will typically provide different descriptions of what constitutes the threat, vulnerability, and risk in this scenario. Some readers describe the frayed rope as a threat, vulnerability, and risk. Similarly, other readers describe the jagged rocks as threat, vulnerability, and risk. The simple fact is that, up to this point, we have not adopted standard definitions for these terms. This lack of agreement on terms is important when trying to communicate effectively, especially with executive management.

The Open FAIR taxonomy introduces a standard set of definitions for these terms that will be described in more detail in later sections of this document.

So, what are the asset, threat, vulnerability, and risk components within the bald tire scenario? The definitions and rationale are described more specifically further on, but, simply stated:
- The asset is the bald tire.
- The threat is the earth and the force of gravity that it applies to the tire and rope.
- The potential vulnerability is the frayed rope (disregarding the potential for a rotten tree branch, etc.).

An *asset* is what you want to protect. It can be money, buildings, human life, etc. In the context of information risk, we can define asset as any data, device, or other component of the environment that supports information-related activities, which can be illicitly accessed, used, disclosed, altered, destroyed, and/or stolen, resulting in loss.

The question is often asked whether corporate reputation is an asset. Clearly, reputation is an important asset to an organization, yet it does not qualify as an information asset given our definition. Yes, reputation can be damaged, but that is a downstream outcome of an event rather than the primary asset within an event. For example, reputation damage can result from public disclosure of sensitive customer information, but the primary asset in such an event is the customer information.

A *threat* acts directly against the asset. The threat can steal money, burn buildings, and kill people; etc. A reasonable definition for threat is anything (e.g., object, substance, human, etc.) that is capable of acting against an asset in a manner that can result in harm. A tornado is a threat, as is a flood, as is a hacker. The key consideration is that threats apply the force (water, wind, exploit code, etc.) against an asset that can cause a loss event to occur.

Vulnerability is a derived value. An example of a derived value is Speed = Time x Distance. Vulnerability is computed by comparing Threat Capability (Tcap) to Resistance Strength (RS). When Tcap is greater than RS we are "vulnerable". When Tcap is less than RS we are not vulnerable.

You may have wondered why "potential" is emphasized when we identified the frayed rope as a potential vulnerability. The reason it's only a potential vulnerability is that we first have to ask the question: "Vulnerable to what?". If our frayed rope still had a tensile strength of 2,000 pounds per square inch, its vulnerability to the weight of a tire would, for all practical purposes, be virtually zero. If our scenario had included a squirrel gnawing on the frayed rope, then he also would be considered a threat, and the rope's hardness would determine its vulnerability to that threat. A steel cable (even a frayed one) would not be particularly vulnerable to our furry friend. The point is that vulnerability is always dependent upon the type and level of force being applied. Vulnerability is also not simply a Yes or No answer, it is a derived value and assets typically have some level of vulnerability. As an example, consider how vulnerable people are to catching a common cold. It can vary. Different people have various factors that influence how vulnerable they may be (e.g., age, sleep, stress, health, immune system, etc.).

What about risk? Which part of the scenario represents risk? The fact is that there is not a single component within the scenario that can be pointed to and identified as the risk. Risk is not a thing – we cannot see it, touch it, or measure it directly. Similar to speed, which is a derived value, risk is a derived value – risk equals the probable frequency and probable magnitude of future loss – in formal terms risk is derived from the combination of Threat Event Frequency (TEF), Vulnerability (Vuln), and asset value and liability characteristics.

1.1.3 Why use the Open FAIR Body of Knowledge?

The following are five reasons why you should use Open FAIR Body of Knowledge for risk analysis:

1. Emphasis on risk

   Often the emphasis in such analyses is placed on controls; for example, we have a firewall protecting all our customer information – but what if the firewall is breached and the customer information stolen or changed? By using the Open FAIR Body of Knowledge, the analyst emphasizes the risk, which is what management cares about.

2. Logical and rational framework

   It provides a framework that explains the how and why of risk analysis. It improves consistency in undertaking analyses.

3. Quantitative

   It's easy to measure things without considering the risk context – for example, the systems should be maintained in full patch compliance – but what does that mean in terms of loss frequency or the magnitude of loss? The Open FAIR taxonomy and method provide the basis for meaningful metrics.

4. Flexible

   It can be used at different levels of abstraction to match the need, the available resources, and available data.

5. Rigorous

   There is often a lack of rigor in risk analysis: statements are made such as: "that new application is high risk, we could lose millions …" with no formal rationale to support them. The Open FAIR risk analysis method provides a more rigorous approach that helps to reduce gaps

and analyst bias. It improves the ability to defend conclusions and
recommendations.

1.2 The Open FAIR Body of Knowledge

The Open FAIR Body of Knowledge consists of the following Open
Group standards:

- **Risk Taxonomy (O-RT), Version 2.0** (C13K, October 2013) defines
  a taxonomy for the factors that drive information security risk – Factor
  Analysis of Information Risk (FAIR).
- **Risk Analysis (O-RA)** (C13G, October 2013) describes process aspects
  associated with performing effective risk analysis.

The Open Group has also published the following additional risk analysis
guidance, which may be useful to risk practitioners, and provide additional
background information for those seeking Open FAIR Foundation
certification:

- **The Open Group Guide: Requirements for Risk Assessment
  Methodologies** (G081, January 2009) identifies and describes the key
  characteristics that make up any effective risk assessment methodology,
  thus providing a common set of criteria for evaluating any given risk
  assessment methodology against a clearly defined common set of
  essential requirements.
- **The Open Group Guide: FAIR – ISO/IEC 27005 Cookbook** (C103,
  November 2010) describes in detail how to apply the Factor Analysis of
  Information Risk (FAIR) methodology to ISO/IEC 27005.

1.2.1 Relationship to Other Open Group Standards

The Open FAIR Body of Knowledge provides a model with which to
decompose, analyze, and measure risk. Risk analysis and management
is a horizontal enterprise capability that is common to many aspects of
running a business. Risk management in most organizations exists at a
high level as Enterprise Risk Management, and it exists in specialized

parts of the business such as project risk management and IT security risk management. Because the proper analysis of risk is a fundamental requirement for different areas of Enterprise Architecture (EA), and for IT system operation, the Open FAIR Body of Knowledge can be used to support several other Open Group standards and frameworks.

The TOGAF® Framework
In the TOGAF 9.1 standard, risk management is described in Part III: ADM Guidelines and Techniques. Open FAIR can be used to help improve the measurement of various types of risk, including IT security risk, project risk, operational risk, and other forms of risk. Open FAIR can help to improve architecture governance through improved, consistent risk analysis and better risk management. Risk management is described in the TOGAF framework as a necessary capability in building an EA practice. Use of the Open FAIR Body of Knowledge as part of an EA risk management capability will help to produce risk analysis results that are accurate and defensible, and that are more easily communicated to senior management and to stakeholders.

O-ISM3
The Open Information Security Management Maturity Model (O-ISM3) is a process-oriented approach to building an Information Security Management System (ISMS). Risk management as a business function exists to identify risk to the organization, and in the context of O-ISM3, information security risk. Open FAIR complements the implementation of an O-ISM3-based ISMS by providing more accurate analysis of risk, which the ISMS can then be designed to address.

O-ESA
The Open Enterprise Security Architecture (O-ESA) from The Open Group describes a framework and template for policy-driven security architecture. O-ESA (in Sections 2.2 and 3.5.2) describes risk management

as a governance principle in developing an enterprise security architecture. Open FAIR supports the objectives described in O-ESA by providing a consistent taxonomy for decomposing and measuring risk. Open FAIR can also be used to evaluate the cost and benefit, in terms of risk reduction, of various potential mitigating security controls.

O-TTPS
The O-TTPS standard, developed by The Open Group Trusted Technology Forum, provides a set of guidelines, recommendations, and requirements that help assure against maliciously tainted and counterfeit products throughout commercial off-the-shelf (COTS) information and communication technology (ICT) product lifecycles. The O-TTPS standard includes requirements to manage risk in the supply chain (SC_RSM). Specific requirements in the risk management section of O-TTPS include identifying, assessing, and prioritizing risk from the supply chain. The use of the Open FAIR taxonomy and risk analysis method can improve these areas of risk management.

The ArchiMate® Modeling Language
The ArchiMate modeling language, as described in the *ArchiMate Specification*, can be used to model EAs. The ArchiMate Forum is also working to extend the ArchiMate language to include modeling security and risk. Basing this risk modeling on the Risk Taxonomy (O-RT) standard will help to ensure that the relationships between the elements that create risk are consistently understood and applied to enterprise security and risk models.

O-DA
The O-DA standard (Dependability Through Assuredness), developed by The Open Group Real-time and Embedded Systems Forum, provides the framework needed to create dependable system architectures. The requirements process used in O-DA requires that risk be analyzed before

developing dependability requirements. Open FAIR can help to create a solid risk analysis upon which to build dependability requirements.

1.2.2 Relationship to Other Risk Frameworks and Methodologies

The practice of risk analysis and management is supported by a number of industry standards and frameworks. These include general standards and frameworks that deal specifically with enterprise risk management, such as:

- ISO 31000
- COSO Enterprise Risk Management
- SABSA
- COBIT

In addition, there are a number of industry, national, and international standards and frameworks that deal specifically with information security risk analysis and management such as CRAMM, FRAP, OCTAVE, NIST 800-30, and ISO 27001 and ISO 27005. While it is beyond the scope of this section to describe how the Open FAIR standards relate to each of these, Open FAIR supports many of them by providing a consistent means to effectively measure and analyze risk. Open FAIR is most often used to quantitatively measure risk (although it can be used in support of qualitative risk analysis as well). The Risk Taxonomy (O-RT) standard and the Risk Analysis (O-RA) standard describe the "how" of risk analysis at a deeper level than most of these other standards and frameworks, and as such can be used in concert with them to create solid risk analysis in support of risk management programs based on these frameworks. To map specific Open FAIR elements, processes, inputs, and outputs to ISO 27005, The Open Group Security Forum created a detailed mapping guide: the *FAIR – ISO/IEC 27005 Cookbook*.

Chapter 2
Basic Risk Analysis Concepts

This chapter will help you understand the basic concepts of risk analysis.

This chapter includes:
- Basic risk concepts
- The risk management "stack"

2.1 Basic Risk Analysis Concepts

In this section we will introduce the basic concepts used in risk analysis. When we start to talk of measuring risk, particularly quantified measurement, some people raise concerns about whether it can be done. The basic concepts in this section are some of the distinctions we need to make about what we do and do not do, as well as how we do it.

2.1.1 Probability *versus* Possibility

In order to analyze risk it is critical to understand the difference between *possibility* and *probability*. You can think of possibility as being binary – something is possible or it is not. Probability, however, is a continuum that addresses the area between certainty and impossibility.

Since risk is invariably a matter of future events, there is always some amount of uncertainty. This is important because executives cannot choose or prioritize effectively based upon statements of possibility. For example, it is possible that there could be a meteor strike close to where you live; however, the probability of that is very low, so we do not typically consider that when leaving the house each day. Similarly, it is possible for business systems to be compromised but it does not happen with every attack, otherwise there would be no e-business. Effective risk decision-making can only occur when information about probabilities is provided, and when we start to provide that information that is when we start to provide value.

2.1.2 Probability *versus* Prediction

Another important and related distinction is that risk analyses should not be considered predictions of the future. The word *prediction* implies a level of certainty that rarely exists in the real world, and doesn't help people understand the probabilistic nature of analysis. Keep in mind that, as a decision-maker, even though you can't tell me when exactly an event will occur, knowing the probability of it occurring is valuable information.

2.1.3 The Risk Management "Stack"

Without a logical, tightly-defined taxonomy, risk assessment approaches will be significantly impaired by an inability to measure and/or estimate risk factor variables. This, in turn, means that management will not have the necessary information for making well-informed comparisons and choices, which will lead to inconsistent and often cost-ineffective risk management decisions. The relationship between these elements is known as the Risk Management Stack, and can be illustrated as follows:

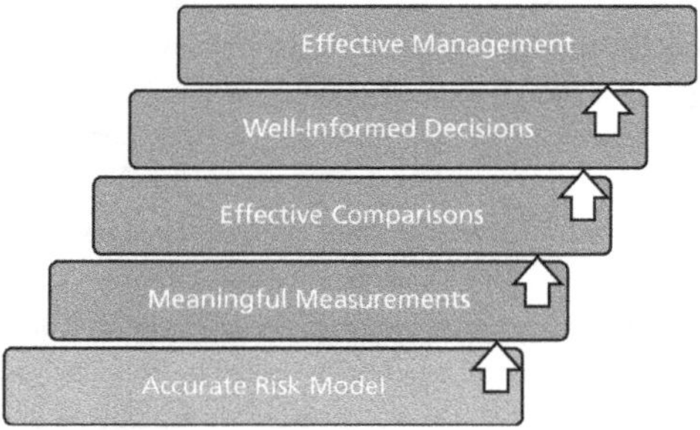

Figure 1: The Risk Management Stack

Chapter 3
Risk Taxonomy

This chapter describes the Open FAIR taxonomy of risk terminology. It describes the factors that drive risk – their definitions and relationships. Each factor that drives risk is identified and defined. Furthermore, the relationships between factors are described so that mathematical functions can be defined and used to perform quantitative calculations.

3.1 Risk

> Risk is defined as the probable frequency and magnitude of future loss (also known as "loss exposure").

The Open FAIR method focuses solely on pure risk (only resulting in loss) as opposed to speculative risk (which might generate either a loss or a profit). With this as a starting point, the first two components of risk are loss frequency and loss magnitude. These are referred to in the taxonomy as Loss Event Frequency (LEF) and Loss Magnitude (LM), respectively, as shown in Figure 2. If either of these components are missing then you are not talking about risk, you are likely talking about a subcomponent of risk. As we cannot predict the future it is also important to recognize that any statement of frequency or magnitude is uncertain and should be expressed as a probable frequency or probable magnitude.

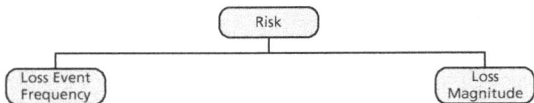

Figure 2: Risk and its components

We will look closer at how these components of risk are further decomposed in detail in the rest of this chapter, starting with an overview of the complete risk taxonomy.

3.1.1 Risk Taxonomy Overview

The complete risk taxonomy is comprised of two main branches: Loss Event Frequency (LEF) and Loss Magnitude (LM). Within those two branches are the factors that drive the occurrence and magnitude of losses. Figure 3 lays out the higher-level abstractions within the framework.

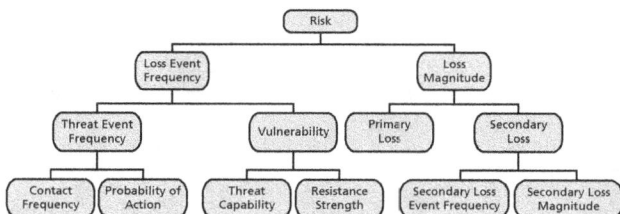

Figure 3: High-Level Risk Taxonomy Abstractions

3.2 Loss Event Frequency (LEF)

> Loss Event Frequency (LEF) is the probable frequency, within a given timeframe, that a threat agent will inflict harm upon an asset.

In basic terms this can be thought of as how often a bad thing happens to something that we care about; for example, your money is stolen, or hackers perform a denial of service attack against your online banking system. See also Section 4.7.

In order for a loss event to occur, a threat agent has to act upon an asset, and that asset must be vulnerable, such that loss results. This leads us to our next two factors: Threat Event Frequency (TEF) and Vulnerability

(Vuln) – when you see an increase in either of these factors then we can expect the LEF to increase as well.

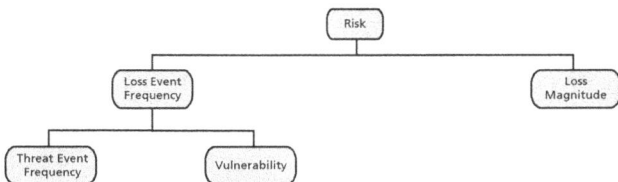

Figure 4: Loss Event Frequency (LEF)

Probability always is based on a timeframe (event X is 10% likely to occur over the next Y) because, given no time-framing, almost any event is possible.

3.2.1 Threat Event Frequency (TEF)

> Threat Event Frequency (TEF) is the probable frequency, within a given timeframe, that a threat agent will act in a manner that could result in a loss.

For example, the probable frequency, within a given timeframe, that a thief tries to steal the money, a tornado hits a building, hackers perform a denial of service attack on your computer system, etc. See also Section 4.2 and Section 4.6.

The value of TEF is expressed as a percentile.

This definition and the definition for LEF are very similar. The only difference is that the definition for TEF does not include whether threat agent actions are successful. In other words, threat agents may act against assets, but be unsuccessful in affecting the asset.

This definition also provides us with the two factors that drive TEF: Contact Frequency (CF) and Probability of Action (PoA). Note that PoA is predicated upon contact. Figure 5 adds these two factors to our taxonomy.

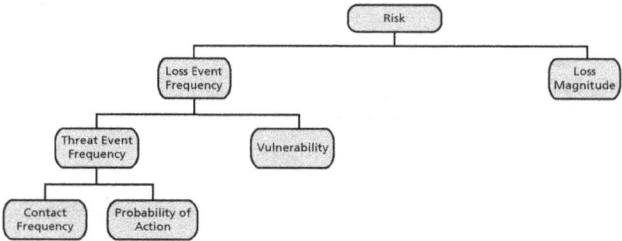

Figure 5: Threat Event Frequency (TEF)

3.2.1.1 Contact Frequency (CF)

> Contact Frequency (CF) is the probable frequency, within a given timeframe, that a threat agent will come into contact with an asset.

The data type is an integer.

Contact can be physical or "logical" (e.g., over the network). Regardless of contact mode, three types of contact can take place, as follows:

- **Random Contact** – the threat agent "stumbles upon" the asset during the course of unfocused or undirected activity.
- **Regular Contact** – contact occurs because of the regular actions of the threat agent. For example, if the cleaning crew regularly comes by at 5:15, leaving cash on top of the desk during that timeframe sets the stage for contact.
- **Intentional Contact** – the threat agent seeks out specific targets.

Each of these types of contact is driven by various factors. An analogy is to consider a container of fluid containing two types of suspended particles – threat particles and asset particles. The probability of contact between members of these two sets of particles is driven by various factors, including:

- Size (surface area) of the particles
- The number of particles
- Volume of the container
- How active the particles are
- Viscosity of the fluid
- Whether particles are attracted to one another in some fashion, etc.

3.2.1.2 Probability of Action (PoA)

> Probability of Action (PoA) is the probability that a threat agent will act against an asset once contact occurs.

Once contact occurs between a threat agent and an asset, action against the asset may or may not take place. For some threat agent types, action always takes place. For example, if a tornado comes into contact with a house, action is a foregone conclusion. Action is only in question when we're talking about "thinking" threat agents such as humans and other animals, and artificially intelligent threat agents like malicious programs (which are extensions of their human creators). As an example, consider a thief and a museum containing valuable antiquities. A thief may be in a museum but choose not to act, he or she may be an art lover or the safeguards may deter them. Just because a threat is in contact does not mean they will always take action.

The PoA is expressed as a percentage.

The probability that an intentional act will take place is driven by three primary factors, as follows:

- **Value** – the threat agent's perceived value proposition from performing the act.
- **Level of effort** – the threat agent's expectation of how much effort it will take to accomplish the act.
- **Risk of detection/consequences** – the probability of negative consequences *to the threat agent*; for example, the probability of getting caught and suffering unacceptable consequences for acting maliciously.

The perceived value of an item can affect the PoA when we are considering "thinking" threat agents. For example, the latest model laptop in plain view in a parked car may be more attractive than an older model and thus there may be an increased PoA.

Different threat agents may have different perceived values of an object; for example, a casual thief may see the value of a laptop as the street price for selling it on, whereas a thief with computer skills may see it as the value of the device and the information contained on it.

The perceived level of effort can also impact the PoA. For example, if the laptop is in an unlocked car then the opportunist thief who tries door handles in a car park is more likely to take action than if the car is locked.

Changes in the perceived level of effort can also impact the PoA. For example, if the thief after stealing the laptop in the car with the intent to steal the information on it, then finds that it has all its information encrypted, then they may decide it is too much effort to attempt to decrypt the information.

Perceived risk to the threat agent can also impact PoA. For example, if the car is parked in a poorly lit road, then that likely has a different PoA to the car being parked in a well lit car park with CCTV cameras.

Changing some of the factors that contribute to PoA may increase it, or decrease it. For example, a new law and aggressive enforcement put in place in a country, where malicious hacking has been rampant, will decrease PoA from this threat community. A configuration error that inadvertently exposes sensitive information in a collaboration platform to the open Internet may increase PoA.

3.2.2 Vulnerability
Having covered the high-level factors that drive whether threat events take place, we now turn our attention to the factors that drive whether the asset is able to resist threat agent actions.

> Vulnerability (Vuln) is the probability that a threat event will become a loss event.

There is no such thing as "a" vulnerability; vulnerability is always expressed as a percentage.

Vulnerability exists when there is a difference between the force being applied by the threat agent, and an object's ability to resist that force. This simple analysis provides us with the two primary factors that drive Vulnerability: Threat Capability (TCap) and Resistance Strength (RS). Figure 6 adds these factors to our taxonomy. We are vulnerable when TCap is greater than RS.

There is no such thing as being more than 100% vulnerable to damage by any specific threat agent/attack vector combination. Vulnerability can exist such that harm can occur from more than one threat agent through more

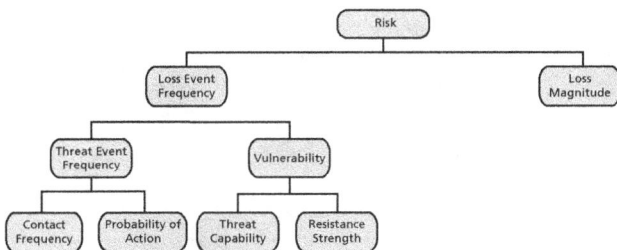

Figure 6: Vulnerability

than one attack vector, but each of those represents a different potential
threat event. For example, if I'm walking down the street at night in a
particularly dangerous part of town, I'm vulnerable to multiple potential
threat events; for example, being run over by a car, being mugged, or
being the victim of a drive-by shooting. The probability of occurrence for
any one of these threat scenarios cannot exceed 100% (certainty) but the
aggregate risk is certainly greater due to the multiple threat scenarios that
could occur.

3.2.2.1 Threat Capability

> Threat Capability (TCap) is the probable level of force that a threat
> agent is capable of applying against an asset.

It is expressed as a percentage value.

Not all threat agents are created equal. In fact, threat agents within a single
threat community are not all going to have the same capabilities. What
this should tell us is that the probability of the most capable threat agent
acting against an asset is something less than 100%. In fact, depending
upon the threat community under analysis, and other conditions within

the scenario, the probability of encountering a highly capable threat agent
may be remote.

As information security professionals, we often struggle with the notion
of considering threat agent capability as a probability. We tend, instead, to
gravitate toward focusing on the worst case. But if we look closely at the
issue, it is clear that focusing solely on worst case is to think in terms of
possibility rather than probability.

When we are estimating the threat capability of a given threat agent
or community, we should consider where they reside relative to the
population of all threats we may face. For example: A malicious internal
system administrator is at the upper end of the capability scale versus
an average employee. This is because privileged insiders like System
Administrators generally have more skills and resources. There can also
be threat capability related to human error scenarios, for example a clerk
mistakenly entering the wrong command or values into a keyboard within
an application leading to a loss event.

Skills

Another important consideration is that threat agents have different skills
(knowledge and experience). Some may be very proficient in applying one
type of force, and incompetent at others. For example, a network engineer
may be proficient at applying technological forms of attack, but may be
relatively incapable of executing complex accounting fraud. Similarly, threat
agents that may be highly adept in working with Microsoft technologies
may be relatively clueless when faced with an older mainframe computer.

Skills are not easily affected – it's not possible to make a threat dumber –
however, we can attempt to reduce their skills by obscuring the asset in
some way.

Resources

A threat agent has two types of resources that can be brought to bear
against an asset. These are time and material.

The resource component of TCap boils down to two elements: time and
materials. In some scenarios it may be possible to affect relative TCap by
either shortening the time available to the threat agent (e.g., by having
highly effective detection and response capabilities) or by minimizing the
materials that are available to them (e.g., removing unnecessary tools and
utilities from systems).

For example, if we have good visibility within our network, we may be
able to reduce the amount of time an external threat may have within our
network prior to being discovered. By reducing the exposure window the
threat may require higher resources in order to affect the asset. Consider, as
a second example, that if we had measures in place to withstand low level
denial of services attacks then the threat would need to bring a higher level
of resources.

3.2.2.2 Resistance Strength

Resistance Strength (RS) is the strength of a control as compared to a
baseline measure of force.

In simple terms, this can be considered the degree of difficulty faced by the
threat agent. For example, a wireless network secured by Wi-Fi Protected
Access II (WPA2) has a higher RS than one secured by Wired Equivalent
Privacy (WEP).

RS is expressed as a percentile.

A rope's tensile strength rating provides an indication of how much force it is capable of resisting. The baseline measure (RS) for this rating in this example is pounds per square inch (PSI), which is determined by the rope's design and construction. This RS rating doesn't change when the rope is put to use. Regardless of whether you have a 10-pound weight on the end of the 500-PSI rope, or a 2,000-pound weight, the RS doesn't change.

Unfortunately, the information risk realm doesn't have a baseline scale for force that is as well defined as PSI. Consider, however, password strength as a simple example of how we can approach this. We can estimate that a password eight characters long, comprised of a mixture of upper and lowercase letters, numbers, and special characters, will resist the cracking attempts of some percentage of the general threat agent population. Therefore, password RS can be represented as this percentile. (Recall that RS is relative to a particular type of force – in this case, cracking.) Vulnerability is determined by comparing RS against the capability of the specific threat community under analysis. For example, password RS may be estimated at the 80th percentile, yet the threat community within a scenario might be estimated to have better than average capabilities – let's say in the 90th percentile range. In this case the TCap of the threat community is larger than the estimated RS and thus we would have a high level of Vulnerability.

3.3 Loss Magnitude

> Loss Magnitude (LM) is the probable magnitude of loss resulting from a loss event.

The previous section – Section 3.2: Loss Event Frequency (LEF) – introduced the factors that drive the probability of loss events occurring. This section describes the other half of the risk equation – the factors that drive LM when events occur.

Out of a population of information security incidents, you will generally have a loss distribution that looks something like Figure 7.

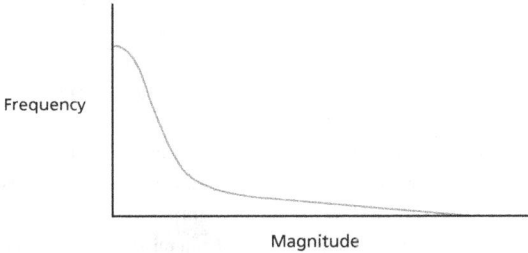

Figure 7: Loss Magnitude (LM) [Source: The Open Group]

In other words, there are far more events that result in loss at the low end of the magnitude spectrum than there are at the high end of the spectrum. For example, individual virus incidents, unauthorized use of systems to serve up MP3 files, even password cracking and loss of Personally Identifiable Information (PII)), rarely result in significant loss. The question we have to ask ourselves is: "Why?". What factors are responsible for this? Clearly some of these events have significant potential for harm, but if we compared the *actual* loss from two similar events – one in which minimal loss occurred, and another where substantial loss occurred – what factors determined the difference? In order for us to make well-reasoned, accurate estimates of loss, we have to understand how loss materializes.

The potential for loss stems from the value of the affected asset(s) and/ or the liability it introduces to an organization. For example, customer information provides value through its role in generating revenue for a commercial organization or services for a public organization. That same information can also introduce liability to the organization if a legal duty exists to protect it, or if customers have an expectation that the information about them will be appropriately protected.

Keep in mind that loss is evaluated from a single perspective – typically that of the organization under analysis. For example, although customers might be harmed if their personal information is stolen, our risk analysis would evaluate the losses experienced by the organization rather than the losses experienced by the customers. See also Section 4.9 and Section 4.10.

3.3.1 Primary Loss

Primary Loss is the direct result of a threat agent's action upon an asset.

The owner of the affected assets would be considered the primary stakeholder in an analysis.

The Open Group is the primary stakeholder in a scenario where its website goes offline as a result of an infrastructure failure. The Primary Loss is based on the direct nature of the asset; for example, how much will it cost to replace a failed component, or how much will it cost to have the IT department put in place additional infrastructure to mitigate for the failure.

Of the six forms of loss described in Section 4.10, Productivity, Response, and Replacement are generally the forms of loss experienced as Primary Loss. The other three forms of loss only occur as Primary Loss when the threat agent is directly responsible for those losses (e.g., Competitive Advantage loss occurring when the threat agent is a competitor, Fines and Judgments loss when the threat agent is filing charges/claims, etc.).

3.3.2 Secondary Loss

> Secondary Loss is a result of secondary stakeholders (e.g., customers,
> stockholders, regulators, etc.) reacting negatively to the Primary Loss
> event.

Think of it as "fallout" from the Primary Loss event. Secondary Loss has
two primary components: Secondary Loss Event Frequency (SLEF) and
Secondary Loss Magnitude (SLM).

An example of Secondary Loss would be customers taking their business
elsewhere after their personal information had been compromised or due
to frustration experienced as a result of frequent service outages.

Of the six forms of loss (see Section 4.10), Response, Competitive
Advantage, Fines & Judgments, and Reputation are most commonly
associated with Secondary Loss. It is unusual to experience Productivity or
Replacement loss within Secondary Loss.

Two important considerations of Secondary Loss are that:
• It is always predicated on a Primary Loss event.
• It does not materialize from every Primary Loss event.

Another important aspect of Secondary Loss is that its effect on an
organization can cascade. As losses pile up from initial Secondary Losses,
additional secondary stakeholders may react negatively, compounding the
effect until losses are so great that the organization fails completely (e.g.,
the demise of Andersen Consulting in 2002).

3.3.2.1 Secondary Loss Event Frequency

> Secondary Loss Event Frequency (SLEF) is an estimate of the
> percentage of time a scenario is expected to have secondary effects.

Although this variable is called a "frequency", it actually is estimated as a
percentage to reflect that it represents the percentage of primary events that
have secondary effects.

3.3.2.2 Secondary Loss Magnitude

> Secondary Loss Magnitude is the losses that are expected to materialize
> from dealing with secondary stakeholder reactions (e.g., Fines &
> Judgments, loss of market share, etc.).

Chapter 4
Risk Terminology

This chapter will help you understand risk terminology. This chapter builds on the terms introduced in the risk taxonomy (see Chapter 3). Without a common understanding of what risk is, what the factors are that drive risk, and a standard use of the terms we use to describe it, we can't be effective in delivering meaningful, comparable risk assessment results. The terms are listed in topic-related order.

4.1 Asset

An asset is anything that may be affected in a manner whereby its value is diminished or the act introduces liability to the owner.

Examples include systems, data, people, facilities, cash, etc.

4.2 Threat

A threat is anything that is capable of acting in a manner resulting in harm to an asset and/or organization.

Examples include acts of God (weather, geological events, etc.), malicious actors, errors, and failures.

4.3 Threat Communities

A threat community is a subset of the overall threat agent population that shares key characteristics.

The threat landscape can be broken down in almost any way that makes sense to help us perform the analysis. Often, a useful approach is to define our threat communities as internal and external threats.

Internal threat communities could include employees, contractors, vendors, and partners.

External threat communities could include cyber criminals (professional hackers), spies, non-professional hackers, activists, nation-state intelligence agencies, and malware.

4.4 Threat Profiling

> Threat profiling is the technique of building a list of common characteristics associated with a given threat community.

Examples of potential threat profile elements or parameters include:
- Motive
- Objective
- Access Method
- Personal Risk Tolerance
- Desired Visibility
- Sponsorship
- Skill Rating
- Resources

The use of threat profiles helps to streamline and improve the consistency of analyses. Threat profiling allows us to ensure all risk analysts share a common definition and assumptions related to threat communities, improving consistency. Enabling the creation of a shortlist of the most probable threat communities to consider reduces the time and effort that might be spent otherwise to analyze every conceivable threat community.

By considering the nature of the threat communities relative to the
industry, organization, and asset, we can come to reasonable conclusions
without falling victim to analysis paralysis.

4.5 Secondary Stakeholders

> Secondary stakeholders are individuals or organizations that may be
> affected by events that occur to assets outside of their control.

For example, consumers are secondary stakeholders in a scenario where
their personal private information may be inappropriately disclosed or
stolen. An example of Secondary Loss would be customers taking their
business elsewhere after their personal information had been compromised.
Other examples of secondary stakeholders could be stockholders,
regulators, etc.

4.6 Threat Event

> A threat event is when a threat agent acts against an asset.

4.6.1 Threat Event Types
In order to develop well-reasoned estimates, it is also important to identify
the type of threat event under analysis.

There are four types of threat scenarios:

1. Malicious
2. Error
3. Failure
4. Natural

An example of a malicious threat event type (where harm is intended) is an attempted theft.

An example of an error threat event type (where an act occurred that was not intended) is entering the wrong command at a keyboard.

An example of a failure event type (where an act resulted in unintended consequences) is where the right command was given, but the system failed to perform as intended.

An example of a natural threat event type (resulting from acts of nature) is high winds.

An example of a non-malicious threat event would be accidentally tripping over a system's power cord. See also Section 3.2.1.

4.6.2 Threat Vector

> A threat vector is the path and/or method used by the threat agent.

In many cases, a final consideration regarding the definition of a threat event under analysis is to identify the threat vector.

For example, an attacker seeking to gain access to sensitive corporate information may try any of a number of vectors – through technical attacks, leveraging human targets, etc. The threat vector describes how they will accomplish their objective, the path they will take. It also known as the "attack vector".

Identifying the relevant vector can be important because each vector may have a different frequency and different control levels. In some cases, threat communities also have different capabilities for different vectors.

The difference between a threat event and a loss event is that the latter only occurs if the former is successful. For example, a hacker may attack a website and be unsuccessful, in which case a threat event has occurred but no loss event.

4.7 Loss Event

> A loss event is when a threat agent's action (threat event) is successful in negatively affecting an asset.

For example, your money is stolen, or hackers perform a denial of service attack against your online banking system.

4.8 Primary Stakeholder

> The primary stakeholder is the person or organization that owns the asset at risk.

For example, The Open Group would be the primary stakeholder in risk scenarios related to its assets.

4.9 Loss Flow

> Loss flow is the structured decomposition of how losses materialize when an event occurs.

The concept of loss flow significantly improves the ability to evaluate Loss Magnitude (LM) (see Section 3.3) accurately.

Loss flow incorporates the following:
• A threat agent acts against an asset.

- This event affects the primary stakeholder in terms of productivity loss, response costs, etc. This is considered the primary component of the loss event.
- Sometimes this initial event also has an effect on secondary stakeholders, such as customers, regulators, media, etc.
- The reactions of the secondary stakeholders may, in turn, act as new threat agents against the organization's assets (such as reputation, legal fees, etc.) which, of course, affects the primary stakeholder. This is referred to as the secondary component of the loss event.

A few things to recognize:
- Secondary Losses are always predicated upon a Primary Loss.
- We may call them "secondary stakeholders" but they are most accurately viewed as "secondary threats" when they begin acting against our assets.

4.10 Forms of Loss

Six forms of loss are defined within the Open FAIR Body of Knowledge, as follows:

1. **Productivity** – generally represents the reduction in an organization's ability to generate its primary value proposition (e.g., income, goods, services, etc.). It can also occur when personnel are operationally unable to perform their duties yet are being paid.
2. **Response** – expenses associated with managing a loss event (e.g., internal or external person-hours, logistical expenses, legal defense, public relations expenses, etc.).
3. **Replacement** – the intrinsic value of an asset. Typically represented as the capital expense associated with replacing lost or damaged assets.
4. **Fines & Judgments** – legal or regulatory actions levied against an organization. Note that this includes bail for any organization members who are arrested. Note that the costs associated with legal defense are captured in response costs.
5. **Competitive Advantage** – losses associated with diminished competitive position. Within this framework, competitive advantage

loss is specifically associated with assets that provide competitive differentiation between the organization and its competition.

6. **Reputation** – losses associated with an external stakeholder's perception that an organization's value proposition is diminished and/or that the organization represents liability to the stakeholder.

4.11 Productivity Loss

There are two types of productivity loss:

- **Reduced revenue** – the reduction in an organization's ability to generate its income, goods, services, etc. This is the type where loss of revenue due to operational outages and discontinuation would be accounted for.
- **Unproductive employee time** – includes the sunk costs associated with personnel who are unable to perform their duties during a loss event but who continue to be paid.

4.12 Revenue Loss

An example of revenue loss would be revenue lost when a retail website is unavailable due to a system outage.

It can be important to distinguish lost revenue from delayed revenue. For example, when a retail website goes down some proportion of its customers may wait to perform their transactions rather than use a different retailer. This, of course, is highly dependent on the nature of the market and competition.

The sales and marketing departments in most organizations will have reliable data to create estimates of lost revenue for such loss events.

4.13 Employee Productivity

An example of resource utilization loss is when a call center's phone lines are down, but personnel continue to be paid.

The human resources, finance, and marketing departments in most
organizations will have reliable data related to the cost of employee time.

4.14 Response Loss

> Response loss is the expenses associated with managing a loss event.

Examples of response loses are internal or external person-hours, logistical
expenses, legal defense, public relations expenses, etc.

The human resources, finance, and marketing departments in most
organizations will have reliable data to estimate the response costs.

4.15 Replacement Cost

> Replacement cost is the intrinsic value of an asset.

Typically represented as the capital expense associated with replacing lost
or damaged assets.

For example, rebuilding a facility, purchasing a replacement laptop,
replacing a terminated employee, covering the losses experienced by fraud,
etc.

4.16 Competitive Advantage Loss

> Competitive advantage loss is the losses associated with diminished
> competitive position.

Within this framework, competitive advantage loss is specifically
associated with assets that provide competitive differentiation between the
organization and its competition.

Within the commercial world, examples include trade secrets, merger and acquisition plans, etc. Outside the commercial world, examples include military secrets, secret alliances, etc.

Common sources include: executives responsible for an organization's strategy, marketing, and sales, as well as an organization's CFO.

4.17 Fines & Judgments (F&J) Loss

> Fines & Judgments loss is the legal or regulatory actions levied against an organization.

This also includes bail for any organization members who are arrested.

Fines are levied by government or regulators. Judgments are the result of civil law suits.

Note that the costs associated with legal defense are captured in response costs.

Examples of F&J loss include:
- Fines levied against an organization by government regulatory agencies for failure to comply with laws related to privacy
- Judgments stemming from civil legal cases
- Settlements stemming from the failure to abide by contractual obligations
- Criminal penalties for the conviction of executives

The regulatory bodies and press are potential sources for F&J data.

4.18 Reputation Damage

> Reputation damage is the loss associated with an external stakeholder's perception that an organization's value proposition is diminished and/or that the organization represents liability to the stakeholder.

From a practical perspective, reputation damage typically materializes as reduced market share (for commercial organizations), reduced stock price (for publically traded companies), reduced willingness to cooperate in joint ventures, or increased cost of capital. Note that this is where a reduction in revenue due to lost market share would be accounted for.

Potential sources for reputation damage data can be found in market share statistics maintained internally or by analyst firms, and company sales data, in both cases combined with pre and post-security breach data values. External data that is useful to understanding potential reputation damage and impact can be found in academic studies, and by analyzing other firm's sales and market capitalizations pre and post-security breach.

4.19 Controls

> A control is any person, policy, process, or technology that has the potential to reduce the Loss Event Frequency (LEF) and/or Loss Magnitude (LM).

At a basic level, there are four ways in which controls can affect risk:

1. **Avoidance controls** affect the frequency and/or likelihood of encountering threats.
2. **Deterrent controls** affect the likelihood of a threat acting in a manner that can result in harm.
3. **Vulnerability controls** affect the probability that a threat's action will result in loss.

4. **Responsive controls** affect the amount of loss that result from a threat's action.

Figure 8 identifies where these control categories play a role within the taxonomy.

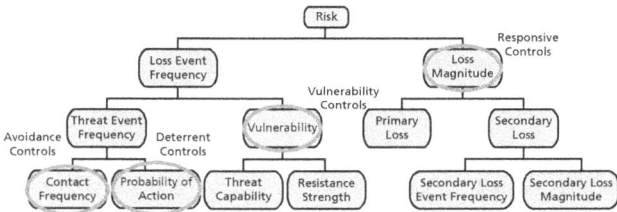

Figure 8: Control Categories

4.20 Avoidance Controls

Examples of information security-related avoidance controls include:

• Firewall filters
• Physical barriers
• The relocation of assets
• The reduction of threat populations (e.g., reducing the number of personnel who are given legitimate access to assets)

As with any control, the effect may not be absolute. For example, firewalls usually are configured to permit certain types of traffic, which means that threat events may still occur against assets behind the firewall. Nonetheless, firewalls also almost invariably reduce the frequency of threat events by shielding against certain types of traffic.

4.21 Deterrent Controls

Deterrent controls reduce the probability that a threat agent will act against the asset in a manner that may result in loss.

Examples of common information security-related deterrent controls
include:
- Policies
- Logging and monitoring
- Enforcement practices
- Asset "hardening" (e.g., many threat actors are opportunistic in nature
  and will gravitate toward easier targets, rather than targets that are
  perceived to be difficult)
- Physical obstacles (e.g., external lights on building, barb-wire fencing,
  etc.)

4.22 Vulnerability Controls

Vulnerability controls reduce the probability that a threat's action will
result in loss. In a scenario where the context is a malicious action,
vulnerability controls are also known as "resistive controls", and they
generally focus on increasing the difficulty a threat actor faces in their
attempts to gain access, disrupt, etc.

Examples of vulnerability controls in an information security context
include:
- Authentication
- Access privileges
- Patching
- Some configuration settings

In a scenario where the context is non-malicious (e.g., human error),
vulnerability controls often focus on reducing complexity and/or difficulty
faced by personnel to reduce the probability that their actions will result
in harm.

4.23 Responsive Controls

Responsive controls refer to those controls that occur after a loss event has been detected and that are focused on reducing the magnitude of loss that results.

Examples of responsive controls in an information security context include:
- Back-up and restore media and processes
- Forensics capabilities
- Incident response processes
- Credit monitoring for persons whose private information has been compromised

Chapter 5
Measurement

This chapter will help you understand how risk elements can be best measured and calibrated. These concepts are fundamental to performing effective risk analysis.

5.1 Calibration

Calibration is a method for gauging and improving an individual's ability to make good estimates. Since measuring risk involves making good estimates, calibration is critical for risk analysts to understand. Performing calibration to make better estimates is a skill that can be learned.

Calibration is key to how FAIR risk analysis works; it uses some of the processes outlined in the book by Douglass Hubbard: *How to Measure Anything*. The key points to the process are:

- Start with the absurd
- Focus on what you *do* know
- Decompose the problem
- Test your confidence
- Think about where you could find data
- Challenge your assumptions

5.1.1 Starting with the Absurd

Calibration starts with making absurd estimates. The purpose of doing this is to enable the risk analyst to recognize starting values for the estimation that are clearly not possible. It is also an attempt to break any bias that an analyst may have.

An example of starting with an absurd estimate would be if you were asked to estimate the wingspan of a Boeing 747 jet, and you provided as an absurd estimate 10' on the low side, and 900' on the high side. Someone with experience seeing the airplanes at airports will recognize that these values are absurd estimates, perhaps using as frames of reference the height of a basketball hoop on the low end, and the length of three football fields on the high end.

Once we understand that these are absurd values for minimum and maximum (min/max) values in a range, we can start to narrow in on values that we'll have more confidence are appropriate as min/max values in a range. So starting with these clearly absurd values, it then becomes possible to narrow in on a more realistic range of min/max values.

5.1.2 Decomposing the Problem

Measurement and estimation in risk analysis requires the analyst sometimes to decompose broad, high-level risk components into smaller pieces that are easier to deal with.

An example of this might be trying to estimate the height of the Willis Tower in Chicago – formerly known as the Sears Tower. By decomposing the problem into "how many floors is the building" and "how much vertical space does each floor occupy", we can start to make sense of the entire question. In information security risk analysis, a similar broad question might be: "How much risk do we have around lost laptops and Personally Identifiable Information (PII)?". To decompose this into components that we can more easily deal with (and for which we might have data to support risk analysis), we can ask ourselves questions such as: "How many laptops have we historically lost each year?", "How much PII is being stored on laptops by employees?", and "What costs do organizations similar to ours experience when they lose PII?".

5.1.3 Testing Confidence using the Wheel

The wheel is a mechanism to help strengthen an analyst's conviction or confidence in an estimated range of values, to move them to a point where the analyst is 90% confident that the actual value is within the min/max range. The wheel mechanism helps risk analysts improve their calibration abilities by forcing them to really evaluate (and revise) their choice for a min/max value in a range.

With an initial absurd range for the value, the next step is to narrow the range to more accurately estimate the actual values so that the analyst is confident that the actual value will fall within the range 90% of the time (a 90% confidence interval).

Hubbard uses the analogy of a wheel to help narrow the range (Hubbard, 2007, p.57ff). The analyst is offered a choice between two scenarios:
1. They will receive $1,000 if the actual value falls within their prediction.
2. Spinning a wheel with 90% of its area painted black and 10% painted red. They will win $1,000 if the wheel stops in the black.

The wheel obviously implements a 90% confidence interval and the desired goal is that the analyst has no preference between the two methods. If the analyst prefers the wheel, then they are not truly confident that their estimate represents a 90% confidence interval for the value and the estimate needs to be revised. The confidence interval can be tightened by asking the analyst to make the same choice regarding whether the estimate will be less than (or greater than) some value 95% of the time.

Making calibrated estimates involves a process that includes:
• Expressing estimates in the form of ranges (e.g., minimum of 1 meter, maximum of 1 kilometer)

- Having initial range estimates that are absurd and then using hard data, soft data, and subject matter expert estimates to narrow the range to a point at which you are 90% in the range's accuracy
- Where appropriate, decomposing the value being estimated into sub-values from which the desired value can be derived (e.g., using the number of stories in a building, and the height of each story, to derive the overall height of a building)
- Leveraging unrelated but familiar references to assist in estimating a desired value (e.g., using the length of a football field as a known distance reference for estimating, for example, the wingspan of an airliner)
- Challenging assumptions underlying the estimates to identify opportunities to improve their accuracy

The following is an example of how to apply the wheel to establish 90% confidence in an estimate. Let us say that you are faced with estimating the frequency of attacks against your company's primary web application.

If we apply the principle of "starting with the absurd" we might use a minimum estimate of one attack every thousand years and a maximum estimate of a billion attacks per year. With this range defined, and with a $1,000 prize at stake, would we prefer to bet on spinning the wheel and landing in the black (a 10% probability) or bet on our range as containing the actual number of attacks the website will experience in the coming year?

Assuming our starting range is truly absurd, there should be no question that our best bet for winning the prize is on the range. From there we begin leveraging whatever hard data (e.g., logs), soft data, and subject matter expertise that might be available to gradually narrow the range.

Each time we narrow the range we ask ourselves again whether we would prefer to bet on the wheel or our range. For example, maybe our first narrowing step is to change the minimum estimate to one attack every one hundred years, and the maximum estimate to a million attacks per year. With that change, do we still prefer our range over the wheel? We continue in this fashion until we get the range to a point where we cannot comfortably choose either the range or the wheel. At that point, you are 90% confident in your estimate.

In some instances, instead of needing to estimate a value where the overall confidence is 90% (i.e., 5% on either end of the range) you may have to estimate a value where only one end of the range is in question. In this instance, you simply change your mental image of the wheel from a 90%/10% division to 95%/5%. In this case, you are adjusting the estimate for only that value in question, and comparing your confidence in that estimate against the odds of spinning the wheel and landing in the 5% section.

5.1.4 Challenging Assumptions
Assumptions may be challenged by getting other analysts' estimates, and by finding data that is useful to the estimation activity. Challenging assumptions is important when estimating because when our assumptions are off, our estimations will be as well.

5.2 Distributions
An Open FAIR risk analysis makes extensive use of distributions when making measurements or estimates. The distributions (description of how often particular values appear in the data) created during such a risk analysis are used to express many of the elements of the Open FAIR risk taxonomy, including (among others) distributions for Contact Frequency (CF), Probability of Action (PoA), Threat Capability (TCap), and Resistance Strength (RS). The advantage to using distributions

versus attempting to derive discrete values is that it is for the most part
impossible to get to a defensible discrete value. We always have some level
of uncertainty in any data and also in information security things change
rapidly. Distributions allow practitioners to express this uncertainty and
change in an effective manner. For example, when estimating attacker
TCap, we typically see a range of different attackers, with different skills
and experience, so using a range is a more accurate way to represent TCap.
The same can be seen to be true for other taxonomy elements such as PoA
and RS. Using distributions in risk analysis helps to provide more accurate
results.

Creating distributions requires the analyst to provide four parameters:
1. Minimum Likely Value
2. Most Likely Value
3. Maximum Likely Value
4. Confidence Level

5.3 Most Likely Values
Within distributions, the value most likely to be observed is the value that
appears most often among all values in the entire data set.

The **mode** is the value that appears most often in a set of data (the most
likely value).

5.4 Monte Carlo Simulations
Monte Carlo simulations are a method for analyzing data that has
significant uncertainty. Monte Carlo simulations perform repeated
random sampling to obtain numerical results. The output of Monte Carlo
simulations used in risk analysis is shown as probability distributions.
Monte Carlo should be considered whenever you wish to apply the Open
FAIR method in a quantitative approach.

The primary advantage of using Monte Carlo simulations in risk analysis is the ability of the method to perform thousands of calculations on random samples, allowing risk analysts to create a more accurate and defensible depiction of probability given the uncertainty of the inputs.

5.5 Accounting for Uncertainty

5.5.1 Range Confidence
Confidence in the end-points of the range is built through training for risk analysts to improve their calibration, and remove their personal estimating bias. The wheel, described in Section 5.1.3, helps to improve calibration and reduce personal bias.

5.5.2 Curve Shaping
Curve shaping refers to the degree of confidence that the analyst has in the most likely value within a distribution. Distributions for which analysts have a very high degree of confidence in the most likely value will be very peaked and narrow, while distributions in which analysts have a low level of confidence in the most likely value will be more flat. An example of a distribution where there is a high degree of confidence in the most likely value might be estimating the range of values for the number of presidential candidates to receive more than 5% of votes. In most modern US elections, there have been exactly two. In terms of how we can increase confidence in the most likely value, we can again use the wheel to move our estimates of most likely values to an improved confidence level for estimates where we don't have significant data.

5.6 Accuracy *versus* Precision
Accuracy can be defined for risk analysis as "our capability to provide correct information", while precision is "exact, as in performance, execution, or amount".

Estimates that are falsely precise can mislead decision-makers into thinking that there is more rigor in the risk analysis than there actually is. Using distributions or ranges can bring higher degrees of accuracy to estimates.

An example of an estimate that is precise but inaccurate would be to estimate that the wingspan of a 747 is exactly 107'.

An example of an estimate that is accurate but not precise would be to estimate that the wingspan of a 747 is between 1' and 1,000'.

The concept of a useful degree of precision refers to creating estimates that have a level of precision that matches the objective of the estimation exercise. To extend the airplane wingspan example, if our range estimate is 10' to 300', and the objective of the estimation exercise is to allow us to build a hangar that will be big enough to house the plane, then the estimate is likely accurate, but it is not usefully precise. What we aim for is accuracy with a useful amount of precision.

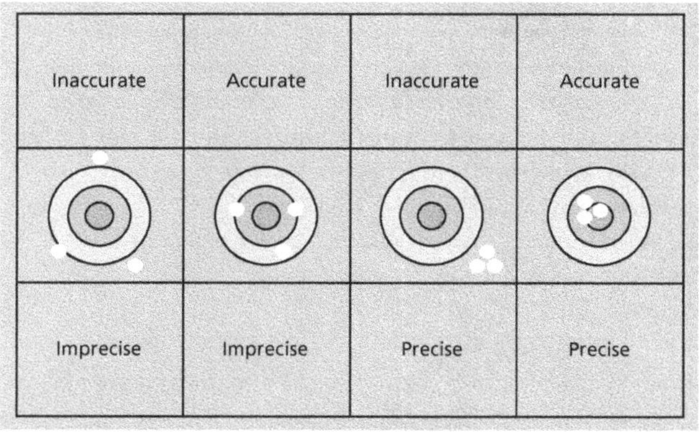

Inaccurate	Accurate	Inaccurate	Accurate
Imprecise	Imprecise	Precise	Precise

Figure 9: Accuracy *versus* Precision[1]

1   Source: CXOWARE Inc.

5.7 Subjectivity *versus* Objectivity

Objective risk measurements are those which are not influenced by personal feelings, interpretations, or prejudice; but which are based on facts and are unbiased. Subjective risk measurements are those that are influenced by personal feelings, interpretations, or prejudice.

Data that is more subjective in nature includes data that is informed primarily by one person's opinion. An information security example might be if we asked a random employee at a company how many laptops the company loses in a given year. Their opinion would be a pretty subjective answer, perhaps informed by their own experience, or their knowledge of co-workers who have lost laptops.

Our goal as risk analysts is to drive objectivity into our risk measurements to the greatest extent possible. We have two primary mechanisms for doing this. The first is to gather more data to help inform the risk estimate. The second mechanism is to develop a better understanding of what the estimates are derived from; in other words, the factors that make up or influence the estimates. The precise definitions and relationships provided in the O-RT standard help to inform this understanding.

Data that is objective in nature, to use the example above, would include going to the IT group in charge of managing IT assets, and asking them for the records of lost laptops for the past several years.

It is important to understand that for many risk measurements, subjectivity and objectivity exist on a spectrum, such that a given measurement is not purely objective or subjective. Purely objective data is not achievable because humans are inherently subjective by their nature. So humans have to decide what data to capture, how to collect it, and what filters to apply to the use and presentation of the data, all of which can (and frequently do) introduce bias.

5.8 Deriving Vulnerability

Vulnerability is the probability that a threat event will become a loss event. In a malicious information security scenario, this translates to the probability that an attacker's Threat Capability (TCap) will exceed the Resistance Strength (RS) of the asset(s) at risk. In the Open FAIR method, Vulnerability is arrived at by:

1. Making an estimate of the threat agent's TCap
2. Making an estimate of RS effectiveness
3. Using Monte Carlo to make random selections from these two distributions and comparing those selections to see whether, in that selection, TCap was greater than RS

If it was, then in that instance the asset was vulnerable. If TCap was not greater than RS, then in that instance the asset was not vulnerable. From the results of thousands of these selections and comparisons, we can determine the percentage of Vulnerability (i.e., where TCap was greater than RS).

5.8.1 Threat Capability (TCap) Continuum

In the Open FAIR taxonomy, Threat Capability (TCap) refers to the level of skills and resources possessed by the potential attacker. Attackers exist on a continuum of skills and resources, including at one end of the continuum attackers with little skill, little experience, and a low level of determination, to the other end with highly skilled, experienced, and determined attackers. This continuum is known as the Threat Capability continuum, and represents the full range of capability of the overall threat population.

The TCap continuum describes attackers as existing at various percentiles, where the 25th percentile are not very skilled, the 50th percentile are mid-level skilled, and the 99th percentile are the most highly skilled.

5.8.2 Defining a Threat Community TCap Distribution

In performing a FAIR risk analysis, the analyst defines a minimum likely capability for the threat, a maximum likely value, and a most likely value. These represent the minimum level of skills that we expect an attacker to have, the maximum level of skills an attacker might have, and the skill level of the most likely attacker. All of these values must be created with a 90% confidence level.

5.9 Ordinal Scales

Using ordinal scales (for example, 0-5) to measure components in a risk analysis, or to categorize overall risk level, brings numerous problems.

These include:
- The meaning of each ordinal value is undefined.
- Ordinal values don't accommodate range values spanning multiple ordinal values. For example, if our ordinal scale starts at 1, defined as range of probability from 1-20%, and 2, defined as 21-40%, how do we deal with a range of probability from 15-35%?
- Ordinal numbers shouldn't (or can't) be multiplied, at least not without creating arbitrary results with little meaning.

Chapter 6
Risk Analysis Process

This chapter will help you understand how we can leverage the FAIR risk taxonomy and terminology to perform the process of risk analysis. In this chapter we draw upon the following example scenario:

> A Human Resources (HR) executive within a large bank has his username and password written on a sticky-note stuck to his computer monitor. These authentication credentials allow him to log onto the network and access the HR applications he is entitled to use.

6.1 Assumptions

It is important to realize that in any risk analysis, regardless of method, assumptions will play a role. Different assumptions will often drive the reasoning for different estimates to be produced by two or more analysts. One area where documenting all assumptions is vital is within the identification of the components (i.e., scoping) of the analysis.

In order to manage this it is important that the analyst clearly documents the key assumptions to ensure all those who review the analysis understand the basis for the values that were used. Assumptions may be challenged by getting other analysts' estimates, and by finding data that is useful to the estimation activity. Challenging assumptions is important when estimating because when our assumptions are off, our estimations will be as well.

6.2 Scoping and Definition

Time and effort spent in scoping is crucial to performing effective analyses. It helps to identify how many analyses need to be performed (see Section 6.2.4). Careful scoping of an analysis will usually result in an overall saving in time spent on the analysis, due to better clarification of data requirements and less time spent troubleshooting and revising the analysis.

If we do not have the analysis adequately scoped out then we can run into many problems; for example, different people may bring different assumptions throughout the process, Loss Magnitude (LM) may be difficult to quantify, and we may not understand or be able to derive the Loss Event Frequency.

6.2.1 Identify the Asset at Risk

The first question we have to answer is: "What asset is at risk?". Another way to think about this is to determine where value or liability exists.

A clear definition of the asset at risk enables a more accurate and precise estimate of the LM.

To understand why having a clear picture of the asset at risk is critical, let's think back to the "bald tire" example. Absent any other assumptions, the asset is the tire. If we put a child in the tire swing, we have an entirely different risk scenario, with very different LM. This is easily extended to IT risk scenarios, where we need to ask ourselves frequently if the asset is the server or laptop, or the frequently far more valuable data residing on the computing device.

In the scenario provided at the start of this chapter we have multiple assets: the credentials as well as the applications, systems, and information that the credentials provide access to. In this case, however, we'll focus on the credentials, recognizing that their value is inherited from the assets they are intended to protect.

6.2.2 Identify the Threat Community

The second question we have to answer is: "Risk associated with what threat?". If we examine the nature of the organization (e.g., the industry it's in, etc.), and the conditions surrounding the asset (e.g., an HR executive's office), we can begin to parse the overall threat population into communities that might reasonably apply. It is recommended to create a short list of the most probable threat communities. By considering the nature of the threat communities relative to the industry, organization, and asset, we can come to reasonable conclusions without falling victim to analysis paralysis.

Within this scenario, it seems reasonable to consider the risk associated with the following threat communities:

- The cleaning crew
- Other HR workers with regular access to the executive's office
- Visitors to his office
- Job applicants
- Technical support staff

With experience it becomes easier to determine which communities are worthwhile to include and exclude. For this example, we'll focus on the cleaning crew. A recommended technique for defining the threat community is to use threat profiling (see Section 4.4).

6.2.3 Identify the Loss Event

The final scoping question we have to answer is: "What does the loss event look like?". Another way to think about this is to clearly define the event that may occur which would result in a loss to the organization. By answering this question we can ensure that all stakeholders are aware of the primary concern or event we are measuring (i.e., managing assumptions).

The specificity of this description is important. Note that it excludes events whereby a cleaning crew member used the credentials to log on and surf the Internet, check their social media accounts, or even send illicit email. It also stipulates that the intent be malicious, which excludes acts of simple curiosity, and involves misuse *versus* destruction. These other scenarios could be separate analyses of their own if they were deemed relevant enough. Could the analysis be more general and include these other scenarios? Yes, but because the frequency and impact of these scenarios may vary significantly, making effective estimates would likely be impractical.

When identifying and defining the loss event on which the analysis will focus, it is useful to consider the threat event type (see Section 4.6). Since we have profiled the threat community, the threat event type further defines the context in which the threat community is likely to affect the asset. Common threat events include: malicious, error, failure, and natural/environmental.

In our example, we could define the loss event as: *the malicious access and misuse of sensitive employee information by one or more members of the cleaning crew, using the executive's log-on credentials posted on a sticky-note.*

The specificity of this description is important when deciding the scenarios to analyze. Note that it excludes events whereby a cleaning crew member used the credentials to log on and surf the Internet, check their social media accounts, or even send illicit email. It also stipulates that the intent be malicious, which excludes acts of simple curiosity, and involves misuse *versus* destruction. These other scenarios could be separate analyses of their own if they were deemed relevant enough.

6.2.4 Scenario Parsing
During the scoping of the analysis we can consider whether to combine multiple scenarios into a single analysis or whether we should decompose

our analysis down to a single scenario. While there are no "rules" on this topic there are some key considerations to share.

Often we may want to perform a single analysis that encompasses more than one threat community or asset. This is generally acceptable but careful consideration should be given if:
• The threats do not share the same objective.
• The threats do not share the same access methods (internal *versus* external human threats).
• There is more than one asset and each one is distinctly different (e.g., location, controls, value).

If any of the cases above are true, the analyst should consider performing more than a single analysis. It often takes less time and is more efficient to perform multiple "simpler" analyses than to try to make estimates for more complex scenarios.

6.2.5 Identify and Clearly Define Scenario Objectives
Identifying and clearly defining scenario objectives is a critical aspect of any risk analysis. We should ensure that this process is completed for each and every analysis and not bypassed or haphazardly completed for the sake of efficiency. As you will see when we start evaluating the factors related to Loss Event Frequency (LEF) and Loss Magnitude (LM), we will be referring to each of these identified components when making estimations.

6.3 Documenting Rationale
When performing an analysis (especially a quantitative-based analysis), the estimates we enter are often only as good as the rationale documented along with them. When performing a risk analysis, we should anticipate that aspects of it might be challenged, especially from stakeholders who have other assumptions or biases. The rationale needs to clearly and concisely define, and must support, any estimates we have entered.

Well-documented rationale should state the source of all estimates. The
source may be systems (e.g., logs), groups (e.g., incident response), or
industry data. Sometimes we just don't have very good data. When a
situation like this arises, it is not the time to try and "hide" it by poorly
documenting the rationale. As credible analysts, we should do just the
opposite.

6.4 Choosing the Abstraction Level

When we look at the Loss Event Frequency (LEF) side of the taxonomy
(see Figure 10) we see a "tree" structure of lower-level factors driving the
elements above. This is a correct interpretation of how the taxonomy
functions. Unfortunately, as a result of this structure, practitioners often
assume they should start deriving LEF by working at the lowest level of
abstraction (i.e., Contact Frequency (CF) and Probability of Action (PoA)).
It is important to remember that analyses can be performed at higher layers
of abstraction.

To leverage the top-down approach we should first consider whether we
are able to make defensible estimations at the LEF itself. A question we
may ask is: "Has this event happened in the last few years. If so, how many
times?". If the loss event we are measuring has occurred in the recent
past then we may be able to put our estimations directly at the LEF. For
example, if we are attempting to estimate how often storms knock out
power to our building; we likely have very objective historical information
over the past five to ten years showing the frequency of such events. By
leveraging this data we can make LEF estimations directly.

Now, if we don't have data on past loss events, or if factors (such as
controls) have changed, we should step down one layer and attempt to
work at Threat Event Frequency (TEF) and Vulnerability (Vuln). Another
additional consideration around which level of abstraction we should work
at is based on the purpose of the analysis. For instance, if we are evaluating

several different control options and are looking to identify which option is most effective from a risk reduction perspective, then deriving Vuln by analyzing Resistance Strength (RS) and Threat Capability (TCap) may be most appropriate.

To recap: the appropriate level of abstraction to use in an analysis will usually be determined by:

- The purpose of the analysis. If the analysis will be performed multiple times to assist in determining the effectiveness of a new control, then we should work at a lower level (e.g., RS) where the change can be more objectively and accurately estimated.
- The type and quality of data at hand and/or the amount of time available to the analyst – deeper levels of analysis take longer.

The benefit of working higher in the taxonomy is increased efficiency, and when there is data it often is more objective in nature.

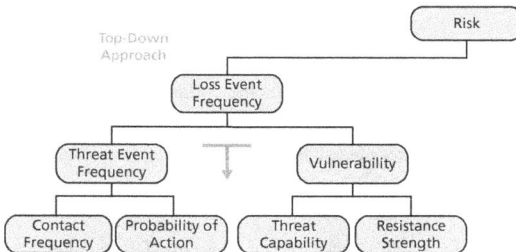

Figure 10: Top-Down Approach

6.4.1 Data Quality
Good data is objective and tracked over a long period of time (shows trending). Poor data is relative, "foggy", one-time captured. Good data is especially difficult to acquire for infrequent events.

Using the Open FAIR method assists with the capture of good data by:

- Defining which metrics are needed
- Providing a model for applying the data so that meaningful results can be obtained

It doesn't, of course, help us with those instances where data isn't available because events are rare. In those cases, regardless of what analysis method is chosen, the estimates aren't going to be as well substantiated by data. On the other hand, the absence of data due to the infrequency of events *is* data – of sorts – and can be used to help guide our estimates. As additional information is acquired over time, it is possible to adjust the initial estimates.

6.5 Finding Data

Common sources for useful information can be data collected by the help desk and IT department, and industry data sources such as DataLossDB. ORG, and the annual Verizon Data Breach Investigations Report.

Good sources of data are ones that are more objective in nature than subjective. This means data which has been observed is often more defensible and credible than data which is opinion-based, although subject matter expert estimates can still be a valuable and credible source of data for analysis.

An example of a question meant to elicit objective data is: "How many laptops did XYZ Corp. lose last year?". A more subjective question would be: "How many laptops do you think XYZ lost last year?".

Objective risk measurements are those which are not influenced by personal feelings, interpretations, or prejudice; but which are based on facts and are unbiased. Subjective risk measurements are those that are influenced by personal feelings, interpretations, or prejudice. Calibrated subject matter expert estimates that are focused on providing unbiased results can be viewed as being more objective than subjective in nature.

6.6 Troubleshooting Analyses

When analysts or stakeholders disagree on the results of an analysis (or a component of an analysis), then there are three recommended techniques that should be used to manage such disagreements.

1. Revisit the scoping and review the assumptions.
2. Leverage the taxonomy.
3. Perform two or more analyses.

The first technique is to revisit the scoping or rationale within an analysis and determine whether an assumption has been made which varies from the other analysts or stakeholders. If a difference is found, this is often easily resolved.

The second technique is to leverage the taxonomy. The taxonomy breaks down the factors that drive risk. For example, if a disagreement exists regarding estimates made at the Loss Event Frequency (LEF), step down to a lower level of abstraction. By stepping one level lower in abstraction both sides may once again find agreement and the higher estimate will now be derived.

The third recommended technique is to perform two or more analyses to encompass the disagreement. As an example, if one analyst believes the Threat Event Frequency (TEF) is at least once a year while a second analyst believes the TEF is less frequent, you can perform two analyses using both figures and observe whether there is a significant deviation in the overall results.

Often you will find that the majority of disagreements will be resolved after approaching the problem using the first two techniques.

6.7 An Example Analysis

We are now going to return back to the scenario introduced at the start of this chapter and look in detail at an example analysis. So far in the earlier sections of this chapter (Section 6.2) we have scoped the analysis. In this section we will describe an analysis performed at a specific level of abstraction in the risk taxonomy. Specifically, it shows deriving Vuln from TCap and RS, and then deriving LEF from TEF and Vuln. It also shows how to evaluate the LM for our example scenario. It finishes by deriving and articulating the risk for this scenario.

6.7.1 Evaluating Loss Event Frequency (LEF)

6.7.1.1 Estimate the Threat Event Frequency (TEF)

A Threat Event Frequency (TEF) estimate is based upon how frequently contact between this threat community (the cleaning crew) and the credentials occurs *and* the probability that they would act against the credentials.

Recognizing that cleaning crews are generally comprised of honest people, that an HR executive's credentials typically would not be considered especially valuable to them, and that the perceived risk associated with illicit use might be high, then it seems reasonable to estimate a Low TEF using the table below.

Rating	Description
Very High (VH)	> 100 times per year
High (H)	Between 10 and 100 times per year
Moderate (M)	Between 1 and 10 times per year
Low (L)	Between 0.1 and 1 times per year
Very Low (VL)	< 0.1 times per year (less than once every 10 years)

Is it possible for a cleaning crew member to have motive, sufficient
computing experience to recognize and leverage the potential value of these
credentials, and a high enough risk tolerance to try their hand at illicit use?
Absolutely! Does it happen? Undoubtedly. Might such a person be on the
crew that cleans this office? Sure – it's possible. Nonetheless, the frequency
is expected to be relatively low given the variables in play.

6.7.1.2 Estimate the Threat Capability (TCap)

Threat Capability (TCap) refers to the threat agent's skill (knowledge
and experience) and resources (time and materials) that can be brought
to bear. In this case, the task is estimating the skill (in this case, computer
skills) and resources (time) the average member of this threat community
can use against a password written on a sticky-note. It's reasonable to
rate the cleaning crew TCap as medium, relative to the overall threat
population, given that basic computer skills are widespread and even the
cleaning crew is likely to have some computer experience. Keep in mind
that TCap is always estimated relative to the scenario being analyzed. If
our scenario were related to a complex technical scenario, such as an SQL
injection attack, we would probably rate the cleaning crew as having a
lower TCap.

Rating	Description
Very High (VH)	Top 2% when compared against the overall threat population
High (H)	Top 16% when compared against the overall threat population
Moderate (M)	Average skill and resources (between bottom 16% and top 16%)
Low (L)	Bottom 16% when compared against the overall threat population
Very Low (VL)	Bottom 2% when compared against the overall threat population

6.7.1.3 Estimate Resistance Strength (RS)

Resistance Strength (RS) has to do with an asset's ability to resist being negatively affected by a threat community. In our scenario, given the combination of credentials being in plain sight and in plain text, the RS is low. An argument could be made for very low, except for the fact that even after logging on the attacker would likely need to navigate one or more applications to find the employee information. This highlights the fact that, in addition to explicit controls, the inherent difficulty in performing an attack will affect the likelihood of its success.

Rating	Description
Very High (VH)	Protects against all but the top 2% of an average threat population
High (H)	Protects against all but the top 16% of an average threat population
Moderate (M)	Protects against the average threat agent
Low (L)	Only protects against bottom 16% of an average threat population
Very Low (VL)	Only protects against bottom 2% of an average threat population

The question sometimes comes up: "Aren't good hiring practices a control for internal assets?" and "Isn't the lock on the executive's door a control?". Absolutely, they are. But these controls factor into the frequency of contact, as opposed to how effective the controls are at the point of attack, because they limit the volume of people who come into contact with the sticky-note.

6.7.1.4 Derive Vulnerability (Vuln)

Deriving Vulnerability (Vuln) is easy once you have established your TCap and RS. Using the matrix below, simply find the TCap along the left side of the matrix, and the RS along the bottom, where they intersect determines the Vulnerability. For our example, as shown below, a medium TCap combined with a low RS results in high Vulnerability.

			Vulnerability (Vuln)			
	VH	VH	VH	VH	H	M
	H	VH	VH	H	M	L
Threat	**M**	VH	H	M	L	VL
Capability	**L**	H	M	L	VL	VL
(TCap)	**VL**	M	L	VL	VL	VL
		VL	**L**	**M**	**H**	**VH**
				Resistance Strength (RS)		

6.7.1.5 Derive Loss Event Frequency (LEF)

Similar to Vulnerability, Loss Event Frequency (LEF) is derived by intersecting the TEF and Vuln within a matrix.

			Loss Event Frequency (LEF)			
	VH	M	H	VH	VH	VH
Threat	**H**	L	M	H	H	H
Event	**M**	VL	L	M	M	M
Frequency	**L**	VL	VL	L	L	L
(TEF)	**VL**	VL	VL	VL	VL	VL
		VL	**L**	**M**	**H**	**VH**
				Vulnerability (Vuln)		

In our scenario, given a TEF of low and Vulnerability of high, the LEF is low. Keep in mind that Vulnerability is a percentage, which means that you can never be more than 100% vulnerable. Consequently, the LEF will never be greater than the TEF.

6.7.2 Evaluating Loss Magnitude (LM)

Using the previous steps, we have determined that the probability of a loss
event in our scenario is low (somewhere between 0.1 and 1 times per year).
Now we're faced with analyzing the magnitude of loss if an event does
occur.

As mentioned earlier, we can reasonably expect these credentials to provide
access to HR organizational information (organization charts, etc.), as well
as employee personal and employment information (performance data,
health and medical data, address, SSN, salary, etc.). For our scenario, we'll
assume that the asset we are most concerned about is personal employee
information.

6.7.2.1 Estimate Primary Loss

Within this scenario, three potential threat actions stand out as having
relevant loss potential, as follows:

- **Misuse** – employee records typically have information that can be used
  to execute identity theft, which introduces potential legal and reputation
  loss.
- **Disclosure** – employee records often have sensitive personal information
  related to medical or performance issues, which may introduce legal and
  reputation exposure.
- **Deny Access (destruction)** – employee records are a necessary part of
  operating any business. Consequently, their destruction can introduce
  some degree of lost productivity.

We'll focus on misuse (e.g., identity theft) in this analysis given that it's
a common concern for scenarios such as this. In some cases it may be
necessary to evaluate the loss associated with more than one threat action
in order to decide which one has the most significant loss potential.

A key assumption in the LM portion of this analysis is that the volume of compromised employee information would be limited to the number of employee records in the system. This is relevant because even a loss of, for example, 15,000 employee records pales in comparison to breaches of customer records, which can number in the millions. Of course, it may also be reasonable to assume that the volume of compromised employee records would be much smaller, due to factors such as:

- Cleaning crew member concerns regarding higher risk from taking more data
- Cleaning crew intent to personally execute identity theft *versus* selling the information for others to abuse

When performing an analysis, the analyst needs to develop rationale that supports their foundational assumptions. When using the qualitative values such as in this example, it sometimes makes sense to perform multiple analyses (e.g., one for best-case, another for most likely, and a third for worst-case). If the analysis is being performed using PERT distributions and Monte Carlo, instead of the matrices used in this document, all three cases can be covered at once.

Our next step is to estimate the Primary Loss magnitude for misuse.

Loss Forms					
Productivity	Response	Replacement	Fines/ Judgments	Comp. Adv.	Reputation
L	M	—	—	—	—

The scale below represents one possible set of ranges to characterize LM. The ranges within scales like this will need to reflect the loss capacity and tolerances of the organization.

Magnitude	Range Low End	Range High End
Severe (SV)	$10,000,000	—
High (H)	$1,000,000	$9,999,999
Significant (Sg)	$100,000	$999,999
Moderate (M)	$10,000	$99,999
Low (L)	$1,000	$9,999
Very Low (VL)	$0	$999

Note that we didn't estimate LM for Replacement, Fines & Judgments, Competitive Advantage, or Reputation. Given the definitions for Primary and Secondary Loss, as well as the individual definitions for each of these loss forms, some of these loss forms may be relevant for Secondary Loss (covered shortly) in this scenario. However, those forms of loss should not materialize directly as a result of the event and thus would not be accounted for in Primary Loss.

Our estimates for Primary Loss in this scenario are based on the following rationale:

- **Productivity** – Although there may be some amount of disruption to the organization, there is no operational outage associated with this scenario and the organization should continue to be able to deliver its goods and services to its customers.
- **Response** – Primary response costs in this scenario are limited to person-hours involved in the investigation, any costs related to dealing with the agency that provides the cleaning crew, as well as any forensic expenses that might arise. A common source for this data would be other incidents the organization may have experienced or, in some cases, industry data.

Note that the rationale above is based on *what is expected to* happen *versus* best and worst-case. This highlights the fact that ordinal matrices tied to numeric ranges are limited in how effectively they represent the full range of possible outcomes. If the analyst wants to evaluate the worst-case proposition, they can do so. In doing so, however, it is critical that they also reflect the (generally) much lower frequency of such an outcome. As mentioned elsewhere, PERT distributions and Monte Carlo provide greater flexibility and analytic power, particularly with regard to capturing the high and low ends of the possible outcomes.

6.7.2.2 Evaluate Secondary Loss

The first step in evaluating Secondary Loss is to identify which, if any, secondary stakeholders would be relevant to the scenario. In other words, identify who, outside of the organization, might react negatively in a manner that would generate additional loss. For a financial institution, the most common secondary stakeholders of interest are customers, regulators, and shareholders.

In this scenario, regulators may react negatively to an event where a large loss of employee-sensitive information was compromised, at least in part because of questions the event might raise regarding controls over customer information. How severely they react will likely be a function of their perception of the existing overall control environment. If you were doing this analysis at a real organization, you would know (or could find out) what the regulatory view of the organization was, which would help you to accurately estimate this source of loss.

Since customer information is not involved in this scenario, we could reasonably assume minimal, if any, negative reaction from customers. Likewise, a compromise of employee information is unlikely to generate much concern with shareholders because the event does not reflect badly on the fundamental value proposition of the institution.

Although most risk scenarios will not treat employees as secondary stake-holders, this is an exception. The affected employees could potentially leave the organization and/or file lawsuits, so it is reasonable to treat them as secondary stakeholders.

6.7.2.3 Estimate Secondary Loss Event Frequency (SLEF)

Once we have established which secondary stakeholders are relevant, we need to estimate the likelihood that they would be engaged, potentially generating various forms of Secondary Loss.

We can use the scale below to select the probability of secondary stakeholder engagement:

Rating	Description
Very High (VH)	90% to 100%
High (H)	70% to 90%
Moderate (M)	30% to 70%
Low (L)	10% to 30%
Very Low (VL)	0% to 10%

Because this event involves the compromise of personal information, it is virtually guaranteed that one or more of the secondary stakeholder communities would be informed and have to be "managed". Consequently, we would rate the probability of secondary involvement as very high.

To derive an actual frequency from that probability estimate, we reference the probability estimate against the primary Loss Event Frequency (LEF) value determined earlier in the analysis:

Primary Loss Event Frequency (LEF)		Secondary Loss Event Frequency (SLEF)				
	VH	M	H	VH	VH	VH
	H	L	M	H	VH	VH
	M	VL	L	M	H	VH
	L	VL	VL	L	M	H
	VL	VL	VL	VL	L	M
		VL	L	M	H	VH

Secondary Loss Probability

6.7.2.4 Estimate Secondary Loss Magnitude (SLM)

The next step is to estimate the most likely LM resulting from misuse for each loss form. This is where assumptions regarding the volume of compromised sensitive information become critical. For this analysis we will assume that all 15,000 employee records are taken. The rationale behind this assumption is that if someone is going to take the personal risk of performing this sort of illicit action, they are likely to try to maximize the value proposition. We could choose to make a different assumption (e.g., a smaller event) if we wanted to but, as with any key assumption in an analysis, we would need to support it with defensible rationale or data.

Loss Forms					
Productivity	Response	Replacement	Fines/ Judgments	Comp. Adv.	Reputation
—	M	—	L	—	—

Magnitude	Range Low End	Range High End
Very High (VH)	$10,000,000	—
High (H)	$1,000,000	$9,999,999
Moderate (M)	$100,000	$999,999
Low (L)	$10,000	$99,999
Very Low (VL)	$0	$9,999

Our rationale for these estimates includes:

- **Response** – In this scenario, response costs include executive time spent in meetings, notification costs, credit monitoring, and expenses associated with inside and outside legal counsel. A specific breakdown is:
  - **Executive time**: 40 hours @ $300 per hour = $12,000
  - **Notification costs**: $5 per employee
  - **Credit monitoring**: $25 * 15,000 employees * 5% acceptance rate = $18,750
  - **Legal expenses**: $100,000
  - **TOTAL**: $200,000 (approx.)
- **Fines/Judgments** – Provided that the company was not negligent in handling the event, and made a concerted effort to protect employee interests, Fines & Judgments should be moderate (if any at all).

No productivity loss occurred because the organization is still able to provide its goods and services.

No material reputation damage is expected to occur because it was an internal event, no customers were affected, and the organization had a security program in place that included policies and education. If, however, the organization had a problematic relationship with its employees or community, an argument could be made that the employee turnover and challenges with hiring could result, the effects of which could be characterized as reputation damage.

No damage to competitive position would occur because their competitors would not have improved their products and services, nor did the products and services of the organization diminish.

Note that if any employees actually suffered loss through identify theft, it is possible that the organization would have to cover those losses. In such a case, those losses would be accounted for as secondary replacement costs.

6.7.3 Deriving and Articulating Risk

Because we separately evaluated Primary and Secondary Loss Event
Frequency (LEF) and Loss Magnitude (LM), we have to derive primary
and secondary risk, and then derive overall risk as a combination of the
two.

6.7.3.1 Derive Primary Risk

We've already done the hard part, as risk is simply derived from the LEF
and probable LM.

Assuming that the scale below has been "approved" by the leadership of
our fictional bank, we can determine that primary risk associated with this
scenario is medium based upon a low LEF (between 0.1 and 1 times per
year) and a moderate probable LM (between $10K and $100K).

Primary Risk

		VL	L	M	H	VH
	VH	M	H	VH	VH	VH
Primary	H	L	M	H	VH	VH
Loss	M	VL	L	M	H	VH
Magnitude	L	VL	VL	L	M	H
(LM)	VL	VL	VL	VL	L	M
		VL	L	M	H	VH

Primary Loss Event Frequency (LEF)

6.7.3.2 Derive Secondary Risk

The process for deriving secondary risk is identical to primary risk, except
we'll use the SLEF (low) and secondary LM (significant) values.

Secondary Risk

Secondary Loss Magnitude (LM)					
VH	M	H	VH	VH	VH
H	L	M	H	VH	VH
M	VL	L	M	H	VH
L	VL	VL	L	M	H
VL	VL	VL	VL	L	M
	VL	L	M	H	VH

**Secondary Loss Event Frequency
(SLEF)**

6.7.3.3 Derive Overall Risk

The last step is to combine primary and secondary risk into an overall risk
value using the matrix below.

Overall Risk

Secondary Risk					
VH	VH	VH	VH	VH	VH
H	H	H	H	H	VH
M	M	M	M	H	VH
L	L	L	M	H	VH
VL	VL	L	M	H	VH
	VL	L	M	H	VH

Primary Risk

A couple of important points to note:
• Cells in the matrix that intersect similar levels of risk (e.g., high primary
  risk and high secondary risk) could be shown as the next higher level of
  risk. In other words, the cell that intersects high risk for both primary
  and secondary could be labeled "VH" and colored red; i.e., interpreting
  that two high-risk conditions result in very high overall risk. This
  is a conservative view, which may be appropriate depending on the
  organization's risk tolerance.
• Qualitative statements of risk (e.g., high, medium, etc.) should reflect
  the loss capacity and subjective risk tolerance of the organization. For

example, the scale below essentially can be interpreted to mean that loss exposures of greater than $10M will be considered "very high" risk and typically treated as such through the application of resources to mitigate the exposure. Organizations of different sizes and risk tolerances will define a different scale.

Magnitude	Range Low End	Range High End
Severe (SV)	$10,000,000	–
High (H)	$1,000,000	$9,999,999
Significant (Sg)	$100,000	$999,999
Moderate (M)	$10,000	$99,999
Low (L)	$1,000	$9,999
Very Low (VL)	$0	$999

In a real evaluation of a problem like executive credentials on a sticky-note, it's likely that we would analyze and report on more than one scenario (e.g., another threat community), and then aggregate the results to have a more complete picture of the true loss exposure.

Chapter 7
Risk Analysis Results

This chapter will help you understand the various aspects of interpreting and communicating FAIR risk analysis results.

7.1 Interpreting Results

The results of a quantitative Open FAIR risk assessment are often generated in tabular format. The table below presents the summary statistics of the resultant distributions computed using Monte Carlo. An example of this output is presented below:

	Minimum	Average	Mode	Maximum
Primary				
Loss Events/Year	0.05	0.17	0.14	0.43
Loss Magnitude	$70,805	$393,005	$441,760	$784,037
Secondary				
Loss Events/Year	0.02	0.07	0.05	0.17
Loss Magnitude	$248,815	$3,689,381	$1,102,702	$17,564,462
Total Loss Exposure	$28,319	$316,229	$172,200	$1,908,713

This table shows the minimum, average, mode, and maximum risk values for both the Primary and Secondary Loss and frequency factors. The frequency is shown as the number of loss events per year, the magnitude is shown as a monetary value. Interpreting this table would be done as follows:

Primary Loss Events/Year
The Primary Losses would occur as little as once in 20 years (0.05) and as much as 43 times in 100 years (0.43). The average frequency is as much as

17 times in 100 years (0.17), but the most likely (mode) value is 7 times in 50 years (0.14).

Primary Loss Magnitude
The Primary Losses, per event, would be as little as $70,805 (minimum) and as much as $784,037 (maximum). The average losses are $393,005, but the most likely losses (mode) are $441,760.

The Secondary Loss events/year and LM are interpreted in the same fashion as the primary factors.

The Total Loss Exposure is the total computed risk that is experienced on an annual basis (if a risk is not shown to be occurring at least once per year). This means that the amount of a single loss event is spread over the years leading up to it. Risk scenarios with loss events occurring once or multiple times per year show the sum of the annual loss events.

Practical advice for communicating results from an Open FAIR risk assessment is to focus on most likely and maximum values, and generously round off the results to whole numbers. For instance, the above table could be interpreted as about $175,000 of annualized loss occurring about once every 7 years (it helps to convert the decimals back into fractions to express the frequency values).

Note that it can also be useful in many instances to communicate both the annualized loss exposure (e.g., $172k average) and the single event LM (e.g., $1.1M average) to help executives get a clear picture of the risk.

7.2 Communicating Results

7.2.1 Applying Qualifiers to Results

Sometimes, quantitative results don't communicate everything that may be necessary in order for well-informed decisions to be made.

Within the Open FAIR taxonomy, two qualifiers have been identified that can help decision-makers understand subtle considerations that are not reflected in numeric data:
• Fragile qualifier
• Unstable qualifier

The fragile qualifier is used to represent conditions where LEF is low in spite of a high TEF, but only because a single preventative control exists. In other words, the level of risk is fragile based on a single point of failure.

For example, if a single control was all that kept malware-related losses low, then that could be said to be a fragile condition.

The unstable qualifier is used to represent conditions where LEF is low solely because TEF is low. In other words, no preventative controls exist to manage the frequency of loss events.

An example might be the risk associated with rogue database administrators. For most organizations, this is a low LEF condition but only because it is an inherently low TEF scenario.

These qualifiers are intended to compensate for the fact that in some scenarios if a decision-maker only looked at the low LEF, they may be lulled into a sense of security that is not warranted.

7.2.2 Translating Quantitative Results into Qualitative Statements

One of the advantages of quantitative risk analysis is that numbers are dispassionate and, by themselves, neutral to bias. Of course, there are instances in which decision-makers don't want to take the time to personally interpret the significance of quantitative results, and just want a simple red, yellow, or green label to look at. Fortunately, it can be relatively simple to convert numeric values to qualitative statements. The caveat is that these translations should be guided by scales that have been approved by management. It is inappropriate for risk analysts to define and use qualitative scales that represent their risk tolerance or their personal interpretation of what they believe the organization's risk tolerance to be.

The challenge, of course, is that management may not be readily available to formally define risk scales. In this circumstance, the analyst may define a scale they believe is accurate for the organization and then have the scale reviewed by management for approval.

An example scale is shown below:

Label	Average Annualized Loss Exposure
Severe (SV)	> $10,000,000
High (H)	$1,000,000 to $9,999,999
Moderate (M)	$100,000 to $999,999
Low (L)	$10,000 to $99,999
Very Low (VL)	< $10,000

If an analysis resulted in an average annualized loss exposure of $4.5M, that could be interpreted as high risk based on this scale.

7.2.3 Capacity and Tolerance for Loss

Capacity for loss is an objective measure, whereas tolerance for loss is subjective.

An organization's capacity for loss can be interpreted as an objective measure of how much damage it can incur and still remain solvent. For many organizations, this is a function of its capital reserves and other tangible resources, as well as its position in the market. For example, an organization with a stockpile of resources has a greater capacity to absorb disruption in its supply line than one that operates on a razor's edge regarding resource availability.

An organization's tolerance for loss can be interpreted as its leadership's subjective tolerance for loss. Although there often is a strong correlation between objective capacity for loss and subjective loss tolerance, there can be significant differences if executive management is personally loss averse. For example, a financial institution may have substantial reserves and a resilient market presence and yet act as though it is highly averse to loss because executive management experienced a personally traumatizing loss in some past position with a different organization.

Ultimately, it is the combination of capacity for loss and tolerance for loss that determines how an organization perceives and responds to risk.

Appendix A
Open FAIR Certification

This appendix provides a summary of The Open Group FAIR
Certification Program for People.

A.1 The Open Group FAIR Certification Program

Certification is available to individuals who wish to demonstrate they have
attained the required knowledge and understanding of the Open FAIR
Body of Knowledge.

There are two levels defined for Open FAIR certification:
- Level 1: Open FAIR Foundation
- Level 2: Open FAIR Certified (future)

For the initial launch of the program certification is available at Level 1
only. The program will be extended in the future to include a second
level. This appendix covers Level 1 – Open FAIR Foundation. Studying
for Open FAIR Foundation can be used as a learning objective towards
achieving Open FAIR Certified, as the learning outcomes in Open FAIR
Foundation will be required for Open FAIR Certified.

A.1.1 Certification Document Structure

The documents available to support the program are as shown in Figure 1:
Certification Document Structure.

Program description documents, such as the Study Guide, are intended
for an end-user audience including those interested in becoming certified.
The program definition documents are intended for trainers, examination

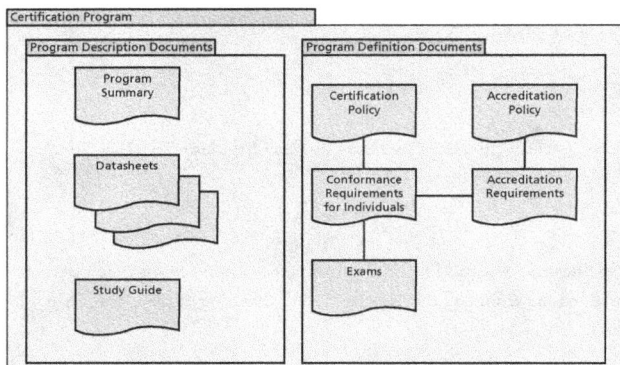

Figure 1: Certification Document Structure

developers, and the Certification Authority. All these documents are available from The Open Group website.[1]

Why become Certified?

Becoming certified demonstrates publicly that you understand the Open FAIR Body of Knowledge as an open, industry standard method for risk analysis. The Open Group publishes the definitive directory of Open FAIR certified individuals and issues certificates.

A.1.2 Open FAIR Foundation

The purpose of certification for Open FAIR Foundation is to provide validation that the candidate has gained knowledge of the fundamentals of the Open FAIR Body of Knowledge, including knowledge of the terminology, structure, and basic concepts; also understanding of the core principles of risk analysis using FAIR, the Risk Analysis (O-RA) standard,

---

1 Available from the Open FAIR certification website at: www.opengroup.org/certifica-
tions/openfair or from The Open Group Bookstore at www.opengroup.org/bookstore.

and the Risk Taxonomy (O-RT) standard sufficient to be able to contribute to a risk analysis project. The learning objectives at this level focus on knowledge and comprehension. Certification for Open FAIR Foundation is achieved by passing the Open FAIR Part 1 Examination. This is a simple multiple-choice examination with 80 questions.[2]

The target audience for certification at this level is as follows:
- Individuals who require a basic understanding of FAIR, the Risk Analysis Standard, and the Risk Taxonomy Standard
- Professionals who are working in roles associated with a risk analysis project, such as those responsible for planning, execution, development, delivery, and operation
- Risk analysts who are looking for a first introduction to FAIR, the Risk Analysis Standard, and the Risk Taxonomy Standard
- Risk analysts who want to achieve Level 2 (Advanced) certification (when available) in a stepwise approach

A.1.3 Open Fair Foundation Certification Syllabus Overview
Individuals certified for Open FAIR Foundation will have demonstrated their understanding of:
- The basic concepts of risk analysis
- Risk terminology, including both taxonomy and terms
- Developing and interpreting FAIR risk analysis results
- The process of risk analysis
- The Open Group FAIR Certification Program

---

2 For the latest information on examinations, see the Open FAIR certification website at: www.opengroup.org/certifications/openfair.

A.1.4 The Certification Process

An overview of the certification process for Open FAIR Foundation is shown in Figure 2 Certification Process (using ArchiMate® notation). The process for becoming certified as shown in Figure 2 is as follows:

1. Candidate wishes to become certified.

   To achieve Open FAIR Foundation certification, candidates must possess a thorough knowledge and understanding of those elements

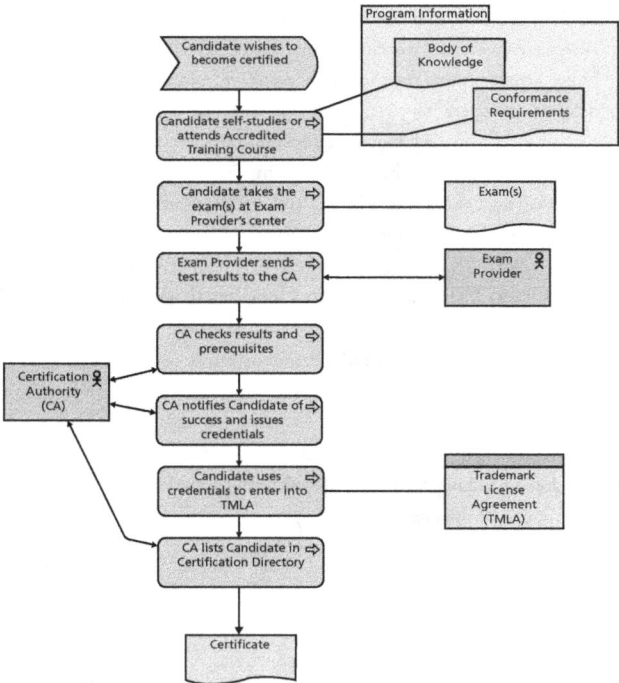

Figure 2: Certification Process

of the Open FAIR Body of Knowledge identified in the Conformance Requirements as being mandatory.

2. Candidate self-studies or attends ATC.
   A candidate can self-study or attend an ATC (Accredited Training Course). The two key inputs to the learning process are the Open FAIR Body of Knowledge itself and the Conformance Requirements. The Conformance Requirements identify which elements of the Open FAIR Body of Knowledge must be known to achieve certification.

3. Candidate takes the examination(s) at Examination Provider's test center.
   Certification is achieved by passing the applicable examination(s) delivered at The Open Group Examination Provider's test center. Candidates who fail to meet the required pass mark will be informed of this and are encouraged to undergo further study and re-sit the examination at a later date. Candidates who fail an examination are not allowed to re-sit an examination again for a period of one (1) month.

4. Certification Authority (CA) checks results and prerequisites.
   Examination results of all Candidates are sent to the Certification Authority for review. The Certification Authority will check to ensure that the pass mark has been met. The Certification Authority will also ensure that Candidates have not failed an examination within the previous month.

5. CA notifies candidate of success and issues credentials.
   The Certification Authority will notify the candidate in writing of the decision. If the decision is to accept the application for certification, the Certification Authority will also issue credentials to the successful candidate that will enable the candidate to access the CA's website to

accept the terms of, and enter into, a Trademark License Agreement (TMLA) with the CA.

6. Candidate uses credentials to enter into Trademark License Agreement.
   The candidate then uses the credentials to access the CA's website to enter into a TMLA with the CA and to obtain the artwork of the applicable Program Logo.

7. CA lists candidate in Certification Directory.
   The CA will then make a Certificate available to the candidate in electronic form and enter the candidate's Certification Record into the Certification Directory. The credentials also allow the Certified Person to control to whom the Certification Record is disclosed and to update contact and employer information in the Certification Record.

A.1.4.1 Open FAIR Part 1 Examination Coverage by Topic

The Open FAIR Foundation certification syllabus is contained in Appendix B. Certain topic areas are weighted as more important than others and thus have more questions. The topic areas covered by the examination together with the number of questions per area in the examination are provided in Table 2. It should be noted that Unit 6 is non-examinable.

Table 2: Open FAIR Part 1 Examination Coverage

Unit	Topic	No. of Questions
1	FAIR Risk Analysis Concepts	4
2	Open FAIR Terminology	28
3	Interpreting and Communicating Results	8
4	FAIR Risk Analysis Process	20
5	Measurement	20
6	The Open Group FAIR Certification Program	0

Appendix B
Glossary

Asset
Anything that may be affected in a manner whereby its value is diminished or the act introduces liability to the owner.

Calibration
A method for gauging and improving an individual's ability to make good estimates.

Competitive Advantage Loss
The losses associated with diminished competitive position.

Contact Frequency (CF)
The probable frequency, within a given timeframe, that a threat agent will come into contact with an asset.

Control
Any person, policy, process, or technology that has the potential to reduce the Loss Event Frequency (LEF) and/or Loss Magnitude (LM).

Fines & Judgments Loss
The legal or regulatory actions levied against an organization.

Loss Event
When a threat agent's action (threat event) is successful in negatively affecting an asset.

Loss Event Frequency (LEF)

The probable frequency, within a given timeframe, that a threat agent will inflict harm upon an asset.

Loss Flow

The structured decomposition of how losses materialize when an event occurs.

Loss Magnitude (LM)

The probable magnitude of loss resulting from a loss event.

Probability of Action (PoA)

The probability that a threat agent will act against an asset once contact occurs.

Primary Loss

The direct result of a threat agent's action upon an asset.

Primary Stakeholder

The person or organization that owns the asset at risk.

Productivity Loss

Represents the reduction in an organization's ability to generate its primary value proposition.

Replacement Cost

The intrinsic value of an asset.

Reputation Damage

The loss associated with an external stakeholder's perception that an organization's value proposition is diminished and/or that the organization represents liability to the stakeholder.

Resistance Strength (RS)
The strength of a control as compared to a baseline measure of force.

Risk
The probable frequency and magnitude of future loss (also known as "loss exposure").

Replacement Loss
The intrinsic value of an asset.

Response Loss
The expenses associated with managing a loss event.

Secondary Loss
A result of secondary stakeholders (e.g., customers, stockholders, regulators, etc.) reacting negatively to the Primary Loss event.

Secondary Loss Event Frequency (SLEF)
An estimate of the percentage of time a scenario is expected to have secondary effects.

Secondary Loss Magnitude (SLM)
The losses that are expected to materialize from dealing with secondary stakeholder reactions (e.g., Fines & Judgments, loss of market share, etc.).

Secondary Stakeholders
Individuals or organizations that may be affected by events that occur to assets outside of their control.

Threat
Anything that is capable of acting in a manner resulting in harm to an asset and/or organization.

Threat Capability (TCap)

The probable level of force that a threat agent is capable of applying against an asset.

Threat Community

A subset of the overall threat agent population that shares key characteristics.

Threat Event

When a threat agent acts against an asset.

Threat Event Frequency (TEF)

The probable frequency, within a given timeframe, that a threat agent will act in a manner that could result in a loss.

Threat Profiling

The technique of building a list of common characteristics associated with a given threat community.

Threat Vector

The path and/or method used by the threat agent.

Vulnerability (Vuln)

The probability that a threat event will become a loss event.

Index

www.ingramcontent.com/pod-product-compliance
Lightning Source LLC
Chambersburg PA
CBHW070408200326
41518CB00011B/2117